THE RISING SON

THE MANIFESTATION

OF

THE SONS OF GOD

By

Richard W. Rundell

The Rising Son: the Manifestation of the Sons of God
Copyright ©, 1996 Richard W. Rundell
ISBN # 0-89228-117-0

Published for the author by
Impact Christian Books, Inc.
332 Leffingwell, Suite 101,
Kirkwood, Mo. 63122

The Author wishes to express his gratitude to the following Bible Publishers for granting permission to quote from their works:

Wm. H. Eerdmans Publishing Co.: *The New Testament: An Expanded Translation* by Kenneth S. Wuest. Copyright 1961. All Rights Reserved.

HarperCollins Publishers: for selections from *The Bible: A New Translation* by James Moffatt. Copyright 1935 by Harper & Brothers. Copyright renewed 1962 by James H.R. Moffat.

The Lockman Foundation: for Scripture taken from the *Amplified ® New Testament,* © Copyright The Lockman Foundation 1954, 1958, 1987. Used by permission; and for Scripture taken from the *New American Standard Bible ®,* © Copyright The Lockman Foundation 1960, 1962, 1963, 1968, 1971, 1972, 1973, 1975, 1977. Used by permission.

Thomas Nelson, Inc. Scripture quotations marked "NKJV" are taken from the *New King James Version.* Copyright 1979, 1980, 1982 by Thomas Nelson, Inc. Used by permission. All rights reserved.

Concordant Publishing Concern for permission to quote from the *Concordant Literal New Testament.*

Zondervan Publishing House. Scripture quotations marked (AMP) are taken from the Amplified Bible, Old Testament. Copyright © 1965, 1987 by The Zondervan Corporation. Those marked (NIV) are taken from the Holy Bible, New International Version ®. NIV ®. © Copyright 1973, 1978, 1984 by International Bible Society. Used by permission of Zondervan Publishing House. All rights reserved.

TABLE OF CONTENTS

Acknowledgements

I wish to thank my pastor, **Gary Parson**, of Redemption Life Tabernacle in Haskell, Ok for his consultation in writing this book, and for the encouragement, prayers and support of those in the body of Christ.

Introduction

Since the dawn of time man has anticipated and sought after his future and his destiny. Now in our time (the last days) his destiny has found him. The Son, the Lord Jesus Christ, now rises. He is now rising in the hearts and lives of mankind, that is, the believers, in their everyday lives, in ever increasing splendor and glory.

The people of the world know intuitively that they are on a collision course with death. Most however, do not realize that they are already "living" or existing in death. Yet their inner being is waiting with great anticipation, an expectancy of something to change that death trap, and that something is *life, life eternal*, through Jesus Christ.

The manifestation of the sons of God brings them hope. It's when those lively stones come together, firmly knit, that the corporate son begins to take form. This form takes on the nature and the character of THE SON.

Chapter 1

First The Natural

1 Co. 15:46 KJV, *"Howbeit that was not first which is spiritual, but that which is natural; and afterward that which is spiritual."*

First the natural then the spiritual. Once you comprehend the natural, you can then more rapidly and properly comprehend and apply it to the spiritual.

Gen. 1:16-18 NKJV, *"Then God made two great lights: the greater light to rule the day, and the lesser light to rule the night. He made the stars also. God set them in the firmament of the heavens to give light on the earth, and to rule over the day and over the night, and to divide the light from the darkness. And God saw that it was good."*

Notice especially the word **"rule."**

Two great lights -- The sun represents the Lord Jesus Christ, the light of the world. It also represents the called out ones, the light of the world, the overcomers who rule the Day with Jesus. They have been called out of darkness into His marvelous light (Col. 1:9-13). The moon represents powers (rulers) of darkness; it has only reflected light or light void of life.

The Sun speaks of the influence of the Kingdom of God

while the moon speaks of the influence of the kingdom of darkness. *"Divide the light from darkness."* Light speaks of spiritual knowledge or understanding, darkness of the lack of understanding.

The energy of the sun rules or controls life on earth. Life is not possible without that energy of the sun. Likewise, spiritual life in man is not possible without the power (energy) of the Holy Spirit actively working in man (Acts 1:8). The rule of the sun determines by seasons the light intensity, the boundaries of any given species of plant or tree where and how it will grow.

The tribe of Judah pitched their camp facing the East; (Judah means praise). Therefore, Judah was the first to see the rising of the sun. So those who praise the Lord are the first to see the rising of the SON and the manifestation of the sons of God in the new day.

The rising of the sun speaks of a new day, a new beginning; old things (old days) are passed away. Just as the natural sun, as it rises, begins to dispel the darkness, so the SON, as He rises in manifestation, begins to dispel the spiritual darkness in the earth.

In the dawning of the day, as the sun comes over the horizon, there is a gradual increase of light until the full brightness of the noonday sun. So shall be the manifestation of the Sons of God - a process that intensifies as Jesus Christ reveals Himself **to** the sons and **through** the sons to the world.

Technically, the sun does not rise upon the earth but the earth revolves toward the sun. But the Scriptures speak of the "rising of the sun"; this term is used nine times in the KJV of the Bible. (i.e. Nu. 2:3; Josh. 12:1; Ps. 50:1; Ps. 113:3; Mk. 16:2). Furthermore, the term, "dawning of the

10

day" occurs four times. These Scriptures most generally speak of a new day or a new time period.

Hosea declared in 6:1-2 KJV, "*Come, and let us return unto the LORD: for he hath torn, and he will heal us; he hath smitten, and he will bind us up. After two days will he revive us: in the third day he will raise us up, and we shall live in his sight*"

And in John 2:19-21 KJV, "*Jesus answered (the Jews) and said unto them, Destroy this temple, and in three days I will raise it up. Then said the Jews, Forty and six years was this temple in building, and wilt thou rear it up in three days? But he spake of the temple of his body.*"

In three 24 hour periods His natural body was out of the tomb. But His body in the spiritual is us. Jesus is bringing to reality the prophecy of Joel and He spoke of how He would do it - in the temple of His body. We are that body. We will not be raised in 24 hour segments, but in the third day we will rise, not from gravity but will be revived. Peter wrote, "*But, beloved, be not ignorant of this one thing, that one day is with the Lord as a thousand years, and a thousand years as one day*" (2 Pe. 3:8 KJV). Thus, there is a natural day of 24 hours, a spiritual day of one thousand years.

Man does not sense or orient himself to revolve around in space every 24 hours toward the sun, but rather to the rising of the sun. Now, man does not revolve toward God or to the Lord Jesus Christ, but The Christ arises in the heart of the believer. In 2 Pe. 1:19 KJV we read, "*We have also a more sure word of prophecy; whereunto ye do well that ye take heed, as unto a light that shineth in a dark place, until the day dawn, and the day star arise in your hearts:*"

11

In Acts 1:11 KJV we read, *"Which also said, Ye men of Galilee, why stand ye gazing up into heaven? this same Jesus, which is taken up from you into heaven, shall so come in like manner as ye have seen him go into heaven."* Jesus left the earth or visible realm rising, so He comes rising in the hearts of believers, not just in the salvation experience but He continues to rise in manifestation to each one.

It is to this "Rising Son" and to the rising of the corporate son or the manifestation of the sons of God, that this book is directed.

At the brightness of the sun, even before it appears on the horizon and begins to bring light to the earth, there is an expectancy, an anticipation, and surety it will rise. We know it has risen without fail for thousands or millions of years ever since the beginning of time. It is totally predictable. It ushers in another segment of time - the day, which is an integral part of the seasons, years, and centuries. Man's life is measured by years. The **sun** rules the day.

Again we read, *"...that one day is with the Lord as a thousand years, and a thousand years as one day"* (2 Pe. 3:8). So today, the day in which we now live (two thousand years from Jesus Christ), is the dawning of the rule of the SON - the beginning of the seventh thousand-year-day since Adam, or the third since Jesus Christ.

While the sun rules, you can build structures or walls to try to keep it out or build solar equipment, mirrors etc. to direct or magnify it, but the sun will still rule. You can build spiritual walls, a wall of rebellion, a wall of apathy, or a wall of self, to try to keep out the SON, but His power and rule remain in both the heavens and in the earth (Rev.

20:6). The Scriptures declare it and man will not stop Him.

"*Set **them** to rule over the day, over the night.*" We are subject to the sun. We can't order the sun to shine one second sooner or at some other angle than it does. Our body, and its biological functions are subject to the day and night hours; we need that sunshine. The plants are subject to the sun for photosynthesis, length of day, even seed production. etc., and for some plants, dormancy in winter, which is subject to the rotation of the sun and the seasons. The type of crops or gardens we plant are also subject to where we live in relation to the sun.

The sun's distance from the earth (93 million miles) ensures that energy reaches the planet at a rate sufficient to sustain life and yet not so fast that the earth and its water would boil away and the molecules of life unable to form. Life is not possible without the energy of the sun. Likewise spiritual life is not possible without the power (energy) of the Holy Spirit, acting and working in man. This is Christ in you.

In Col. 1: 25-27 KJV, we read, *"Whereof I am made a minister, according to the dispensation of God which is given to me for you, to fulfil the word of God; Even the mystery which hath been hid from ages and from generations, but now is made manifest to his saints: To whom God would make known what is the riches of the glory of this mystery among the Gentiles; which is Christ in you, the hope of glory:"*

"In that day you shall know experientially that I am in my Father and you in me and I in you" (Jn. 14:20 Wuest Expanded). *"I in them and thou in me..."* (Jn. 17:23). And Eph. 3:17, *"That Christ may dwell in your hearts by faith..."*

The sun knows it is the center and the earth revolves around it. But the moon wants us to believe the earth is the center for it revolves around the earth. In like manner, the Lord Jesus is our focal point and center. Therefore the gospel of the kingdom is Christ centered, not man centered.

Just as the natural sun rules the earth, now the SON, Jesus Christ, is to rule and reign in a different dimension. How does He rule? According to the Word of God, through the sons of God. Where does He rule or reign? In the earth. First of all, He rules in the hearts of men (in their earth, Christ in you). It's then through those believers that He is to rule in the earth. Christ in you is the basis for the rulership of the Son. All things are subject to Him (1 Co. 15:28). Eventually every knee shall bow and every tongue will confess that Jesus Christ is Lord (Ph. 2:10-11). The Greek here indicates it has already been accomplished in the heavenly realm and is a voluntary act.

Just as the **sun** brings natural life to plants and animals and to the natural man, so the SON brings spiritual life to mankind via the new birth.

Chapter 2

What Is Meant by
The Manifestation?

Let us look at our key text from several versions:

Ro. 8:19, KJV, *"For the earnest expectation of the creature waiteth for the manifestation of the sons of God."*

NKJV, *"For the earnest expectation of the creation eagerly waits for the revealing of the sons of God."*

Amplified, *"(For even the whole) creation (all nature) waits expectantly and longs earnestly for God's sons to be made known - waits for the revealing, the disclosing of their sonship."*

NAS, *"For the anxious longing of the creation waits eagerly for the revealing of the sons of God."*

Phillips, *"The whole creation is on tiptoe to see the wonderful sight of the sons of God coming into their own."*

Concordant Literal N.T., *"For the premonition of the creation is awaiting the unveiling of the sons of God."*

Wuest Expanded Translation, *"For the concentrated and undivided expectation of the creation is assiduously and patiently awaiting the revelation of the sons of God."*

From Wuest's comment: "That is, the nonrational creation, subject to the curse put upon it because of man's sin, is expectantly waiting for the glorification of the saints, that it may also be delivered from the curse under which it now exists." (p. 138 Vol. 1)

We read in 1 Co. 15:49, NKJV, "*And as we have borne the image of the man of dust, we shall also* (Grk.: let us) *bear the image of the heavenly Man.*"

Concerning the manifestation of the sons of God, especially since the whole world is waiting and groaning, we might ask the key questions, What, why, how, where and when? That is,

WHAT is meant by the manifestation of the sons of God?

WHY did God propose such a manifestation?

WHERE will the manifestation take place?

HOW does the manifestation come about? and

WHEN is such a manifestation expected?

The WHEN we will deal with in a separate later chapter.

What Is Meant by The Manifestation?

The word "manifestation" from Ro. 8:19 comes from *apokalupsis,* an uncovering, a laying bare, from Strong's #602, meaning disclosure:--appearing, coming, lighten, manifestation, be revealed, revelation.

Wuest comments concerning the curse (Ro. 8:18). *"When the curse is completely removed from man, as it will be when the Sons of God are revealed, it will pass from creation also, and for this, creation sighs."* (Vol. 1 p. 138)

The manifestation of the Sons of God is the uncovering or the unveiling of the Christ within. If you are a believer, the real you is not your outward appearance but the new creature within. Paul wrote that you are the temple of the Living God (1 Co. 3:16; 2 Co. 6:16), that we are a new creature in Christ Jesus (2 Co. 5:17) and that you have Christ in you, the hope of glory (Col. 1:27). Jesus said, I will come to you and make my abode in you. John 14:23 KJV, *"Jesus answered and said unto him, If a man love me, he will keep my words: and my Father will love him, and we will come unto him, and make our abode with him."*

Possibly we might look upon Ro. 8:19 like this: "...waiting for the **manifestation of God** through His sons."

The world is waiting, not for a revelation, but for a manifestation of God. We can share our latest revelation with one another to increase our knowledge but knowledge puffeth up. We must manifest the Christ in our everyday lives, that is, allow Him to live His life in us and out through us and walk that out in shoe leather. That is the manifestation.

We go to the Old Testament for a type of manifestation. Joseph, the son of Jacob and Rachel, was a type of Christ. As such a pattern, we see many parallels. He rose from the pit to the prison to the palace - advanced to second in command under Pharaoh. Jesus advanced to sit at the right hand of God. Joseph provided grain for his brothers and family, while Jesus is the bread of life. Joseph did not condemn his brothers for what they had done. Gen. 50:2 KJV, *"But as for you, ye thought evil against me, but God meant it unto good..."* (See also Gen. 45:8). Likewise, Jesus came not to condemn the world (Jn. 3:17).

Joseph ministered to the physical needs of his brethren,

both immediate and in the future. Jesus did likewise. Most important of all, concerning our discussion, Joseph revealed himself to his brothers. Gen. 45:3 KJV, *"And Joseph said unto his brethren, I am Joseph."* He revealed not just his identity as such, but subsequently revealed (manifested, if you will), his character and nature, one of total forgiveness, non-condemning, of love for his brothers. In like manner, Jesus revealed Himself first to Peter (Mt. 16:16) then to the disciples and on the day of Pentecost, as the indwelling Christ, to the 120 in the upper room, then to the 3,000 (Acts 2:41). Now through the Christ in us, He is revealing Himself to humanity.

Joseph's brothers sat at the King's table and ate the king's food (Ge. 43:31-34). Food from the king's store-house had previously been sent with them. Jesus invites us to eat the King's food, the Word of God. Joseph served to his brothers. In a like manner, the Holy Spirit serves or reveals to us the Word of God (Jn. 14:26).

Benjamin, Jacob and Rachel's other son of true birth, as all other sons and daughter were from Leah and concubines, and therefore half brothers and sister, received five portions of food (Ge. 43:34), more than he could possibly eat. Five is the number of grace. All that we receive from our elder Brother is by grace. This is a true type of the sons getting extra portions.

What is the food in the banquet that Jesus Christ now sets before us? Jesus declared that His food was *"...to do the will of Him that sent me"* (Jn. 4:34). The food set before us is that we might possess the ability to do His will, and to complete the restoration of all creation.

Mal. 4:2 KJV, *"But to you who fear My name The Sun of Righteousness shall arise With healing in His wings;*

18

And you shall go out And grow fat like stall-fed calves."
Here we see a type of the revelation of the Son, Jesus
Christ, rising in the hearts of men.

Likewise, the Old Testament points to Jesus Christ: His
resurrection from the dead was at a precise time in the
history of mankind. Jesus was to appear at an appointed
time (Hab. 2:3; Heb. 10:37). The "it" of Habakkuk became
the "He" of Hebrews. Jesus Christ, the promised Seed of
the woman (Gen. 3:15) would come at the proper time to
be planted in the earth. It's from that earth that He would
rise via Resurrection Life. Gal. 4:4 KJV, *"But when the
fullness of the time was come, God sent forth his Son,
made of a woman, made under the law."* Isa. 40:5 KJV,
*"And the glory of the LORD shall be revealed, and all
flesh shall see it together: for the mouth of the LORD hath
spoken it."*

The Resurrection

The dawning of a new day, the resurrection of Jesus
Christ, was the greatest event, not only in the history of
mankind, but in the history of the universe. We also note
that His resurrection was at the rising of the sun (Mk.
16:2). And he Himself is the resurrection (Jn. 11:25).

When Jesus rose from the grave, He brought that
resurrection life to man. We have that resurrection power
and life now. We are now walking in a heavenly realm with
the Father. We are seated with him in the heavenlies (Ep.
2:6). That is a present reality. As He is, so are we. That
same power that raised Jesus from the dead now dwells in
us. (Ro. 8:11).

A new era, a new day in the spiritual life of mankind

was to begin in 50 days after the resurrection, on the day of Pentecost, when the Lord Jesus Christ would not just be **among** men, as He was in His earthly ministry, but would be **in** man. (Lu. 17:21; Mt. 3:2; 1 Co. 3:16)

He then began to rise and manifest Himself within and through man - within man's very being. Through the power of the indwelling Spirit of Christ, a new day commences to rise out of man's spiritual darkness into the kingdom of light. For every believer, it's a new day, a new beginning, the day he is born again or born from above (Jn. 3:3)

In the natural, that which is born first is the head, then the body. Spiritually, that which rises first is the head, then the body. First the resurrection of the Head, Jesus Christ, then the resurrection of the many-membered body. In a like manner, first the manifestation of Jesus Christ the head, then the manifestation of the many-membered body.

In Acts 3:2 we read of the man lame from his mother's womb who asked Peter and John for alms. Man is unable to walk spiritually from the time of his natural birth (1 Co. 2:14). Now Acts 3:6 (NKJV), *"Then Peter said, 'Silver and gold I do not have, but what I do have I give you: In the name of Jesus Christ of Nazareth, rise up and walk.'"* Moffatt: v. 6, But Peter said, *"I have no silver or gold, but I will give you what I do have."*

"I'll give you what I do have." What did Peter have? He had the life of Jesus Christ within him, a life that brings total healing of body, soul and spirit. It's not just a life to possess for ourselves but a life to give to others. In the manifestation of the sons of God, the life, nature and character of Jesus are given to us and we are to give all we have to others.

Acts 3:7 KJV, *"And he took him by the right hand and*

20

lifted him up, and immediately his feet and ankle bones received strength." As Christ is manifested through the sons of God and they give out life to the world, their (the world's) feet and ankle bones receive strength. The feet and ankles speak of spiritual understanding, thus the ability and strength to walk out the things of God in their everyday lives. The right hand speaks of ministry and service. "Lifted him up" speaks of lifting people up out of their bondage, out of their earthly way of living, lifting them up to a higher dimension in God. Silver and gold, or the things of the earth perish.

Peter gave life. He gave life to every cell of that man's body and every parcel of his mind. Likewise Jesus never grasped the power, glory and even the life of God the Father for Himself but gave that life to others. Yet He thought it not robbery to be equal with God (Ph. 2:6). We are not to hang onto the power of God for ourselves but give that life to others.

Manifestation includes those who may be different in doctrine or politics or in social or economic status, diverse in many ways, but they live and walk in one accord. They have the mind to do the right thing, to live righteously, and to love their brothers. That's the manifestation of the sons of God. There is diversity in the body, yet our minds are open to the various shades of doctrine. We can get together in diversity without fighting. God is bringing us, with our diversity, together in manifestation.

You can't get a firstfruits company walking in the spirit until they lay aside their natural, that is, their natural desires, ways of living, living by the senses. And you can't have peace until you lay aside war. (Beat their swords into plowshares: Isa. 2:4). When a people who are called by

His name will humble themselves and pray, then He will heal their land. (2 Chr. 7:14). That land is our body and total being.

So many are looking for some Jesus to run around and empty hospitals or people who will walk through walls. They are watching for signs, miracles and phenomenon. That's not necessarily manifestation. Not that some could do that. But that is not the thrust of the manifestation. Furthermore you don't build a church on signs and miracles but by the Word of God and faith in God and by relationships established among God's people. We don't discount signs and miracles but they must be in proper balance.

Manifestation is not what some people think - that we are out to smack the present administration and set up a kind of government in Washington, get us debt free and put a Cadillac in everyone's garage, or wave a magic wand to make you 33 years old. That's wishful thinking and a clever ruse to get you off the spiritual track.

When God moves by manifestation, man comes in with duplication. Anytime man treads God's miraculous manifestation into a carnal realm, it is antichrist. When a thing of God is done by God in purity, there is nothing wrong with that. For example, when the spirit of laughter hits a person or group, if it's really of God, there is nothing wrong. But when you have ten services in a row with nothing but laughter, then we question if God is in it. This is probably a clever trick to get you sidetracked.

There has to be substance, balance and validity to what we do and the way we worship God. Sons manifest through validity, through foundation, and through substance.

The kingdom of God comes not by observation. You

have to be in the spirit to know what is going on. As the millennial reign unfolds, you will see the whole world filled with His glory. It's a matter of attitude, a matter of want to, patience, and all the inner things of the kingdom. That's the manifestation of the sons of God. There is a people who are rising up and who have a right to reign.

Jesus' methods of healing, casting out demons, performing miracles and even paying taxes were simple, without fanfare, without publicity. He sometimes warned them to tell no one what they saw or what He said (Mt. 8:4; 9:30; Mk. 8:26, 30). Jesus made little fuss over anything until he saw the religious people, the Pharisees, in the Temple, where He took a whip and drove out the money changers. Beware of the leaven of the Pharisees.

No Condemnation

The sons of God are supposed to be like Jesus. They do not condemn individuals. Here Jesus did not single out certain Pharisees or Sadducees but came against their system.

Nicodemus came to Jesus by night. Jesus did not condemn him, tell him to renounce the crowd he was hanging out with, or that he needed deliverance from their ways and beliefs. Instead, He presented him with one of the greatest truths of the Bible: *"You must be born again (Gr.: born from above or born anew)"* (Jn. 3:3 KJV).

We don't have to go around telling the world how sinful they are. They know that. We don't have to tell them they are going to hell. They are already in hell, right now. With all the drug and alcohol abuse, corruption, violence, fear to walk the streets at night, fear of financial failures, fear of disease and of dying, broken homes, they are living in hell.

Many live in homes where turmoil reigns. That is hell. Baby boomers in the USA have divorced in record numbers. Thirty six percent of all American children live apart from their fathers. For many of these families, that is hell. Much of the people of the third world countries live in great poverty and in some countries absolute filth. That is living in hell. Hell is not a geographical place. It is a condition. To manifest the Christ, we need not put them in more hell by condemnation, but present to them the Christ in our lives, present to them the plan of salvation, present to them love and mercy.

Chapter 3

Why Did God Propose
Such a Manifestation ?

Why did God propose such a manifestation? It is God's plan and purpose, because He is God, to reveal Himself in the earth. God is spirit. The only way He can reveal Himself thus, is through spiritual man. He first must reveal Himself **in** man, then **through** man to the rest of creation.

Why did God create man? One reason we are born is to become a house of God's habitation. *"Thy kingdom come, thy will be done on earth as it is in heaven"* (Mt. 6:10 KJV). This prayer is an affirmation. The heavenly creation shall rule the earth. God desires that His kingdom manifest in the earth realm, with man himself (Lu. 17:21), where man lives, dwells and where each man relates both to God and to fellow men in perfect union and harmony.

Isa. 45:12-13 (KJV), *"I have made the earth, And created man on it. I; My hands; stretched out the heavens, And all their host I have commanded. I have raised him up in righteousness, And I will direct all his ways; he shall build my city, and he shall let go my captives, not for price nor reward, saith the LORD of hosts."*

Isa. 45:18, (KJV) *"For thus says the LORD, Who created the heavens, Who is God, Who formed the earth and made it, Who has established it, Who did not create it in vain, Who formed it to be inhabited: I am the LORD, and there is no other."*

Man was created for God's pleasure. Ps. 149:4 NKJV, *"For the Lord takes pleasure in His people; He will beautify the humble with salvation." "You are worthy O Lord, to receive glory and honor and power; for You created all things, and by Your will they exist and were created"* (Rev. 4:11 NKJV).

We read from Ge. 1:26-28 (KJV), God's instructions to Adam, "*and* **replenish the earth, and subdue it**..." To *replenish* comes from a Hebrew word meaning to fill. This verse means man is to replenish or fill the earth with the spiritual, that is, to replace all rule by the five senses and by the will of the unregenerated man with that of a spiritual man ruled by the Spirit. It means to restore the earth to its fullness, to reinstate righteousness. Thus, God's plan is to restore all creation into the life of Jesus Christ. This is being done now but yet to be completely fulfilled by and through the Last Adam, Jesus Christ, the Head, along with His body.

Man is spirit, he has a soul and he lives in a body. God did not create Adam or mankind just to float around without a body. But He had a purpose to create the natural body which man possesses. God desired a vehicle or body in which to populate the earth with His nature, His attributes, and His character. That vehicle was man, that is, a spiritual man with a physical body. The first Adam failed the test. Now through the **person of Jesus Christ**, the firstborn of many brethren and through His nature and power indwelling in man, God's desire is coming into fruitfulness. The creation of His image in man is now coming into reality, initially through a firstfruits company (the sons of God).

Man (the first Adam; Gen. 1:27; 1 Co. 11:7) was made in the image of God. The likeness of God was formed in Christ Jesus Who manifested God Himself, not just His image.

Jesus Christ, the express image of God (He. 1:3) came in the form of man, not as an angel, nor any other creature or creation. Think about it. Though God is Spirit, and cannot be seen or touched by the five senses, He chose the form of man, Jesus Christ, **one like ourselves**, in which to manifest Himself.

It's God's purpose that all humanity exhibit the Christ within. All creation can benefit from the manifestation of that divine nature. He wants to release to the earth all that is already accomplished in the heavens. Furthermore, He wishes to establish His covenant in the earth.

One of God's highest purposes is to express Himself in man, not man out in the sky somewhere, but right here on the earth - not just in the distant future but right now. Put another way, God created man to be His expression in the earth. God is to express Himself in man, not in any other creature, not in angels, not in plants or animals, nor as some other religions of the world may teach, in rocks, or inanimate objects. But as the nature of God is expressed in man, man with that nature is one of giving, one who gives the life of God to others.

God's purpose has been to tabernacle with man. After the pattern of Jesus Christ, God chose **man** as the instrument or (earthen) vessel in which to manifest

Himself. It's always been God's plan to be one with man. It's always been His plan to build His kingdom in and through man and that the kingdoms of this world would become the kingdom of the Lord and of His Christ (His anointed) (Re. 11:15).

It's God's purpose to have a family of sons who are just like His first-begotten Son. Jesus came to reveal the Father as He came from the Father (Jn. 16:28). He is likewise the way to the Father. Just before He left the visible world, he said, *"I ascend to My Father and your Father, and my God and your God"* (Jn. 20:17 KJV).

God has been in the past and is now birthing sons who are to bear His image, to be perfect as He is perfect, to manifest the life of the Father just as His Son did. Furthermore, the sons will be able to plant the seed of Jesus Christ in the hearts of the unsaved, something Jesus could not do during His earthly ministry, because He was not sent to do it and did not have the time. That is the job of the sons.

The book of Daniel outlines for us in part the eternal plan and purpose of God as related to mankind: *"But the saints of the most High shall take the kingdom and possess the kingdom for ever, even for ever and ever. And the kingdom and dominion, and the greatness of the kingdom under the whole heaven, shall be given to the people of the saints of the most High, whose kingdom is an everlasting kingdom, and all dominions shall serve and obey him"* (Dan. 7:18, 27 KJV). (See also Ro. 8:16-17; 1 Pe. 2:9).

Jesus Christ fulfills the tabernacle in the wilderness along with its articles of furniture. The ark of the covenant was made of Acacia wood overlaid with pure gold (Ex. 25:11), typifying the human (wood) and the deity (gold) of

Christ, His divine nature being manifested.

In John 10:10 (Amp.) Jesus said, *"...I came that they might have and enjoy life (Zoe), and have it in abundance - to the full, till it overflows."* This speaks of spiritual, heavenly, godly life, not the abundance of material possessions and earthly pleasure. Zoe is life in the absolute sense, life as God has it, that which the Father has in Himself, and which He gave to His Son to have in Himself (Jn. 5:26). Christ in turn is the life of the believer.

Fulfillment in Christ

Eph. 1:10, Phillips translation, *"He purposes in his sovereign will that all human history shall have consummated **in Christ, that everything that exists in heaven or earth shall find its perfection and fulfillment in Him"***

*"And great and important and weighty, we confess, is the hidden truth - the mystic secret - of godliness. **He (God) was made visible in human flesh,** justified and vindicated in the (Holy) Spirit, was seen by angels, preached among the nations, believed on in the world (and) taken up in glory"* (1 Ti. 3:16 Amp.).

God simply descended from the invisible realm of the Spirit, where He had no visible manifestation, and wrapped Himself in a virgin womb. Jn. 1:14 KJV, *"And the Word was made flesh, and dwelt among us, (and we beheld his glory, the glory as of the only begotten of the Father,) full of grace and truth."*

In Jn. 16:14-15 Amp. we read, *"He (The Spirit of Truth - verse 13) will honor and glorify Me, because He will take of (receive, draw upon) what is Mine and will reveal* *(declare, disclose, transmit) it to you. **Everything that the Father has is mine.** This is what I meant when I said that He will take the things that are Mine and will reveal (declare, disclose, transmit) them to you."* The Spirit of Truth (the Holy Spirit) thus reveals to spirit filled believers whatever belongs to Jesus, which is everything the Father has. The believer in turn reveals or manifests such truth to the world.

If Jesus Christ has everything the Father has, then He has all the character, all the attributes, all the authority, all the power in heaven and in earth (Mt. 28:18), and the complete divine nature of the Father. *"For it has pleased [the Father] that all the divine fullness - the sum total of the divine perfection, powers and attributes - should dwell in Him permanently"* (Col. 1:19, Amp.).

He is the head over all things. (Eph. 1:2); He has been given a name above all others (Ph. 2:9); He has been given dominion and position (1 Pe. 3:22); and is sitting at God's right hand (Eph. 1:20).

Transformed Into His Image

The Apostle Paul wrote: *"(For my determined purpose is) that I may know Him - that I may **progressively** become more deeply and intimately acquainted with Him, perceiving and recognizing and understanding [the wonders of His person] more strongly and more clearly. And that I may in the same way come to know the power outflowing from His resurrection [which it exerts over believers]; and that I may so share His suffering **as to be continually transformed [in spirit into His likeness, even]** to His death, [in the hope] that if possible I may attain to*

30

the *[spiritual and moral] resurrection [that lifts me] out from among the dead [even while in the body]"* (Phil. 3:10-11 Amp.). The Concordant Literal N.T.: *"...to the resurrection that is out from among the dead."*

In Jn. 12:3 we read the account of Mary pouring 300 pence worth of ointment on the feet of Jesus. Three hundred is the number of divine deliverance. Jesus Christ, the Head, needs the feet (company) to fulfill His plan and purpose on the earth (1 Co. 12:21). The feet are those in the body of Christ who walk the earth, those who have contact with the earth (that is, those in the earth realm - those of the world who groan for the manifestation of the sons of God)). The ointment speaks of the Spirit. That anointing delivers the Body of Christ from the bondage of corruption (Ro. 8:21).

Ro. 8:28-29 KJV, *"And we know that all things work together (God is in all things that work for you) for good to them that love God, to them that are the called (the Body of Christ) according to his purpose. For whom He did foreknow, he also did predestinate* **to be conformed to the image of His son,** *that he might be the firstborn among many brethren."*

Prophets can speak the word of God and servants can do the will of God but only a son can bear His nature and likeness on the earth - and conform to the image of His Son. That is the purpose of God. God is not interested in what you do but who you are. If you are the right person, with the right nature, you will do the right things. And we can, through the precious promises of God, become partakers of the divine nature of God (2 Pe. 2:4). We will act in love towards our brethren in the Body of Christ and manifest that love to the world, because love (agape) will be a part of our nature. (1 Jn.4:16-17).

While on the earth, Jesus manifested not only each and every attribute of God, but in perfect balance and harmony. This is a present reality as He, now as the indwelling Christ, manifests Himself in believers. Everything that is in Jesus needs to be expressed in manifestation in the earth. The link that binds God and Jesus Christ is spiritual. The link that then binds God to man and Jesus Christ to man is also spiritual and the link that binds the believers together is spiritual (Jn. 17:21). The true church is the habitation of God through the Spirit, the house not made with hands, eternal in the heavens (2 Co. 5:1).

The purpose of the Body of Christ is to reveal the nature of God. He saved us to be conformed to His image in the earth. Jesus Christ, the Pattern, was the fullness of God. No one individual human can reveal all the aspects of God's nature, but each one can manifest an aspect of His nature, i.e. an aspect of His love, an aspect of His gentleness, His peace, His compassion, etc.

Only in Jesus do we see the perfected image of God. Yet, if that's all there was to Christianity, then the Scriptures, especially the New Testament, were written in vain. The resurrected Christ is able to reproduce **Himself,** along with His nature and attributes in mankind.

Chapter 4

Where Will the
Manifestation Take Place?

Jesus came to earth in a body not unlike yours and mine, born not in a king's palace, but of a common family, born of a woman, lived a common life, ministered to and walked among and related Himself to the common man of the day. He ministered to the every day life of man, voluntarily limited Himself to the time and dimensions of man, even the man of that culture and era, and was subject to hunger and tiredness. He came, not as an angelic being, not in a glorified state, but as a common man.

As Jesus walked the earth He lived a life which He said was not His own but the Father within Him. That is, Jesus Christ reached man where man dwelt, in his physical surrounding, in his lack of spiritual understanding, in the sickness of his spirit, soul and body, in the helplessness and bondage of the adamic nature (Ro. 7), in his prison, in his broken heart, to man who was at enmity with God. He preached the gospel of the kingdom which is man's answer to the dilemma he is in. **In short, God would meet man on man's level of living and understanding** (Lu. 4:18), **and would raise him up.**

Likewise the Sons of God have revealed the Christ within themselves (they have since Pentecost) and are now revealing the Christ and shall in the future reveal the Christ. Where? In the earth, in the nitty gritty of everyday life of the common man, in all mankind, in every continent of the earth - not out in the sky somewhere, nor as angelic beings. Christ is revealed through man to man.

Contrary to traditional thought, man can attain to the life of perfection while dwelling on the earth. (Col. 3:14; He. 6:1). God equipped us to go on to perfection. In Jn. 17:23 Jesus declared, *"I in them, and thou in me (the power to accomplish the task), (so) that they may be made perfect (Grk.: perfected) in one and that the world may know that thou hast sent me, and hast loved them, as thou has loved me"* - the reason we are to follow Him to be perfected.

This teaching in the past has placed the ideal Christian life, maturity and perfection in Christ, even the word **"perfection"** upon an unreachable pedestal. It has ventured forth a multitude of excuses why we can't reach it: such as, "We must first die and go to heaven." (There is no scriptural basis for such an expression); "We can't until Christ returns."; "Christ is perfect, therefore we can't be perfect"; or "It is not for this day or this time," or "It's for another people." The result has been that first people give up trying, and become passive in their Christian walk. Second, much of the interpretation of related Scriptures concerning the Christian walk or progress to Christian maturity is distorted, and third, is futuristic, thus robbing us of the *now* reality.

Chapter 5

How Does This Manifestation Come About?

There are an infinite number of processes we must go through so that Christ may be formed in us. Ga. 4:19 NKJV, *"My little children, for whom I labor in birth again until Christ is formed in you."*

The word "formed" comes from the Greek *Morphoo* which suggests a change of character of the outward man to correspond to the inward man. It's a process, such as from a caterpillar to a butterfly. Christ is yet to be formed in His fullness. It's through the power of the Holy Spirit that the Christ be formed in you.

As much as we would like to, we cannot skip any of these processes. God will not allow it. And they will be different for each one of us. Some processes will hurt (largely our flesh) and we would desire to skip over them or to take a short cut.

Without the processing or chastening of a Father, we end up as bastards. Without the processing or tilling of our garden (that's us) we end up with thorns and thistles in our midst. Without adversity, we will not grow. But we will be tried. We will go through a wilderness. We may kick and scream and dig in our heels trying to do our own thing or go our own way, submitting to our own will. Well, do we want to spend forty years or forty days in the wilderness? The choice is ours. We can yield to our own will or to the will of God. Jesus declared, in Mt. 15:13 KJV, *"... Every plant, which my heavenly Father hath not planted, shall be rooted up."* Every nature or adamic thing that God did not introduce, He will root up.

As we go through these processes, our attitude is of utmost importance. Notice, in his prison Epistles, the attitude of Paul toward his own circumstances or consider the time he and Silas prayed and sang praises to God, despite their plight in stocks (Acts 16:24-25). Our attitude in what we are going through is what God grades us on.

1 Co. 15:36 KJV, *"Thou fool, that which thou sowest is not quickened (resurrected), except it die:"* To manifest the life of Christ, we must also manifest His death, not literal death, but our self life has to die or be replaced by the life of Christ. Unless a seed dies, it cannot produce the next generation. (Jn. 12:24).

You **will** manifest the Christ within you. You hear people pray like this, *"Lord, make me more Christlike."* You don't have to pray that you will, you don't have to hope you will, or wish for it. You don't really have to make a conscience effort, or strive to manifest that nature. The Christ Seed within you can produce nothing else It's not a matter of most likely event, nor high probability, but you will, if you are born again and possess the Pentecostal experience, manifest the Christ nature and as you mature spiritually, you will manifest more and more of His nature and His character. Spiritual growth cannot be measured by men's natural measurements - or discerned by the natural mind (1 Co. 2:14) - you cannot see it with the natural eye.

The Amplified in 1 Co. 2:14 states: *"But the natural, nonspiritual man does not accept or welcome or admit into his heart the gifts and teachings and revelations of God, for they are folly (meaningless nonsense) to him; and he is incapable of knowing them - of progressively recognizing, understanding and becoming better acquainted with them - because they are spiritually discerned and estimated and appreciated."* In modern terminology, the natural man does not have a clue to what is going on in the spirit.

If you are a believer, you possess the nature of Christ within, yet you are not going to manifest that nature in your own strength. But there is power and guidance from the Holy Spirit to manifest that nature and that character. (Acts 1:8).

Jesus declared that if He was raised from the earth, He would draw all men unto Him (Jn. 12:32). Likewise as the sons are raised up from the earth realm where they live by the senses, up from their earthly way of thinking and acting, to the Head (Christ), they will draw men to them, who then will begin to see the Christ.

Present your body as a living sacrifice, all your organs of your body for His exclusive use. The Spirit of Jesus Christ has made your body His temple. The life inside of you has been through death, has risen again and conquered death and is now not subject to death. That life is now inside of you. We must realize the reality of that. It is an established fact. We don't have to pray for it or wish for it or ask for it. His deathless life is a part of us and from our spirit flows to every cell, muscle and organ of our body. and out through us, through our eyes, mouth, and hands. That deathless life then flows out to the world. The eyes speak of what we see with spiritual eyes, the mouth of what we say, the hands of what we do. Recognize it. That resurrection life is in every part of our body, including the part that is sick. Out from us flow life. Out of us flow rivers of living water. This is part of the manifestation of the living Christ within us.

Where There Is No Vision, People Perish

Prov. 29:18 (NJKV), *"Where there is no revelation, the people cast off restraint; But happy is he who keeps the law."* KJV *"...no vision, the people perish..."* Moffatt: *"People break loose without a guiding hand...."* The word "perish" from the KJV is Strong's #6544. para', paw-rah'; a prim. root; to loosen; by impl. to expose, dismiss; fig. absolve, begin:--avenge, avoid, bare, go back, let, (make) naked, set at naught, perish, refuse, uncover, perish.

That is, people who have no vision or revelation of God's order, a vision of His divine plan or revelation of life and immortality, cast off restraint. To cast off restraint means that people without this vision, revelation, or guiding hand will break loose, go helter-skelter, vary back and forth from one doctrine or church to the next, one life style to the next, one set of values to the next, without pattern or purpose. Part of that plan and purpose of God is the manifestation of the sons of God.

As Jesus Christ is revealed through the sons, others come in to the knowledge of God and of His Son Jesus Christ. Being born again (Gr.: born anew) is just the first step. They then come into an experiential knowledge - to know by experience - the love and nature of God - that they would grow spiritually, including the Pentecostal

38

experience - that their lives too would be changed - to reflect the life of Jesus within them - this knowledge of life of God spreading to the nations, to the four corners of the earth. We read in Isa. 45:22 KJV, *"Look unto me, and be ye saved, all the ends of the earth: for I am God, and there is none else"*. Mal. 3:12 KJV, *"And all nations shall call ye blessed: for ye shall be a delightsome land, saith the LORD of hosts"*

"He (Christ) comes to be glorified in His saints..." (2 Th. 1:10: NAS). Who is His glory? Jesus, the Pattern Son, was the radiance of His glory and the exact representation of His nature (He. 1:3.NAS) (express image of His person - KJV). In the relation Jesus was to the Father, we are to Him; that is, we are to be His image or representation in the earth. Man is the image and the glory of God (1 Co. 11:7). Ps. 72:19 states: *"...let the whole earth be filled with His glory."* The wise shall inherit glory (Pr. 3:35). Since we are His inheritance, we are to become His glory. The veil has been rent. The sons have entered into the Most Holy Place and will do the works of Jesus and greater works because of the glory in the presence of God in the Most Holy Place. **They will manifest, as Jesus did, the glory of the Father.**

Throughout much of the Bible, God works in threes. Man is a tripartite being. He is a spirit, he possesses a soul (mind, will and emotions) and he lives in a body. God instructed the Israelites that they must observe three feasts in a year. (Passover, Pentecost and Feast of Tabernacles) (De. 16:16). The tabernacle in the wilderness and the temple had three main compartments. The outer court had natural light which corresponds to natural understanding, the salvation experience or the 30 fold (1 to 30) realm.

The Holy Place had the artificial light of the candlestick (lampstand) (Ex. 27:20) and corresponds to the light (understanding) given by the Holy Spirit to the believer who receives the Baptism of the Holy Spirit with evidence of speaking in tongues. This is also called the Pentecostal Experience or the 60 fold (31 to 60) realm.

The Most Holy Place had the divine Light of God, (Lev. 16:2), corresponding to Divine understanding or the 100 fold (61 to 100) realm. It's when the believer who has passed the 30 and 60 fold realms and pressed on into the 100 fold realm that he begins to receive the divine understanding. This is called the Feast of Tabernacles Experience (Lev. 23:34).

Jesus Christ as Head did not attempt nor was His purpose to finish building the Kingdom. The son's task as firstfruits is to build the kingdom and bring the rest of the church into the kingdom who will then bring in the whole world. How? By the manifestation of the Christ within. Christ is now establishing His kingdom within His people, within each and every believer.

Speaking of Christ's body, the church, we read in Eph. 4:13 (Amp.), *"[That it might develop] until we all attain oneness in the faith and in the comprehension of the full and accurate knowledge of the Son of God; that [we might arrive] at really mature manhood - completeness of personality which is nothing less than the standard height of Christ's own perfection - the measure of the stature of the fullness of the Christ, and the completeness found in Him."* And in verse 16, *"For because of Him the whole body (the church in all its various parts closely) joined and firmly knit together by the joints and ligaments with which it is supplied, when each part [with power adapted to its need] is working properly (in all its functions), grows to full maturity, building itself up in love."*

In Isa. 66:1 KJV God declared, *"The heaven is my throne, and the earth is my footstool...."* Heaven represents the ruling element or government, the throne, while the earth represents the element ruled or governed, the portion under subjection, the footstool, the spiritual ruling the natural, the sun over the moon.

Again in Isaiah we read, *"Behold, I create new heavens and a new earth, and the former shall not be remembered, nor come to mind."* (Isa. 65:17 KJV). The new heaven is the new government with the ruling class. At the head will be the Lord Jesus Christ and along with Him are the overcomers who will be priests, judges and saviours.

The chapters that follow expand further on the HOW of manifestation.

Chapter 6

We Must Know God

If we are to manifest God to the world, then we must first truly know God. That is, not know about God, but know God by our spirit. In 1 Jn. 4:6 the Amplified states: *"....Whoever is learning to know God - progressively to recognize and understand God [by observation and experience] and to get an ever clearer knowledge of Him - listens to us; ..."* Here the Greek *ginosko* is translated "knoweth" in the KJV. Vincent comments on this verse: "...he who is habitually and ever more clearly perceiving and recognizing God as his Christian life unfolds. The knowledge is regarded as progressive and not complete."

The unsaved of the world don't want God in their mind or conscience. They want to be free to do their own thing. Christians as well, in the secret areas of their lives, can fall into this trap. Nor are preachers, teachers and students of the Word immune from this problem. Some don't want God to examine their pet doctrines and teachings to see if they truly are of God or if instead they spring from the traditions of men. They don't want God in that area of their mind. They are afraid they'd have to swallow their pride and admit their past teaching was wrong. We must be careful not to be carried about with every wind of doctrine (Eph. 4:14).

In 1 Jn. 2:3 KJV *"And hereby we do **know** that we know him, if we keep his commandments."*

The Amplified (1 Jn. 2:3-4) expresses it, *"And this is how we may discern [daily by experience] that we are coming to know him - to perceive, recognize, understand and become better acquainted with Him; if we keep (bear in mind; observe, practice) His teachings, (precepts, commandments) whoever says, I know Him - perceive, recognize, understand and am acquainted with Him - but fails to keep and obey His commandments (teachings) is a liar, and the truth [of the gospel] is not in him"*

In contrast to all other creatures, God gave man a heart to know Him and a will to obey Him.. To know God is a step by step process, progressively learning to perceive Him, to recognize Him in our everyday lives and to understand Him by (spiritual) observation and experience and by the study of His Word by our spirit. His Word will reveal His nature and His character. Knowing God is a relationship.

1 Jn. 3:6 Amp. declares: *"No one who abides in Him - who lives and remains in communion with and in obedience to Him, [deliberately and knowingly] habitually commits (practices) sin. No one who habitually sins has either known Him - recognized, perceived or understood Him, or has had an experimental* ("experiential" - a more suitable word- this author) *acquaintance with Him."*

The Psalmist David recognized some of the character and nature of God. Ps. 86:5 NKJV, *"For You, Lord, are good, and ready to forgive, And abundant in mercy to all those who call upon You."* Ps. 86:7, *"In the day of my*

trouble I will call upon You, For You will answer me."
And in Ps. 86:15 NKJV, *"But You, O Lord, are a God full
of compassion, and gracious, Longsuffering and abundant
in mercy and truth."* He is a God who helps us and
comforts us (Ps. 86:17).

Deu. 6:4 KJV, *"Hear, O Israel: The LORD our God is
one LORD:"* This means that God is whole, He is complete
in Himself. He need not go outside of Himself to fulfill
Himself. Contrary to what is sometimes taught, God did not
create man because He was lonely. In that sense He would
not be complete.

True love comes not from ourselves or our emotions but
from God. That love grows as we progressively come to
know God. *"Beloved, let us love one another, for love
[springs] from God, and he who loves [his fellow man] is
begotten (born) of God and **is coming (progressively) to
know and understand God** - perceive and recognize and
get a better and clearer knowledge of Him. He who does
not love has not become acquainted with God - does not
and never did know Him; for God is love"* ((1 Jn. 4:7-8
Amp.).

One purpose of knowing God is that we might be
fruitful, and that we might give life to others (1 Pe. 1:5-8).
To know God we must first know His only Son. In fact, the
only way to God is through Jesus Christ.

Jesus told Thomas, *"...I am the Way and the Truth and
the Life; no one comes to the Father except by (through)
Me. **If you had known Me - had learned to recognize Me
- you would also have known my Father.** From now on
you know Him and have seen Him...."* (Jn. 14: 6 Amp.)
God's desire is to have man restored to Himself. To get
that need met, He gave His only Son.

In Jn. 1:18 Amp. we read: *"No man has ever seen God at any time; the only unique Son, the only begotten God, Who is in the bosom [that is, in the intimate presence] of the Father, He has declared Him - he has revealed Him, brought Him out where He can be seen; He has interpreted Him, and He has made Him known."* The Concordant Literal N.T. expresses it *"He unfolds Him."* Moffatt: *"...but God has been unfolded..."* Wuest: "Absolute deity in its essence no one has ever yet seen. God uniquely-begotten, He who is in the bosom of the Father, that One fully explained deity."

Jesus, as He walked the earth and now as the resurrected Lord Jesus Christ, indwelling in us, personifies, that is, interprets, the nature and character and even the purpose of God, revealing Him through us to others. As you would unfold a piece of paper, unfolding speaks of a progressive, greater and greater revelation of God, from the part toward the whole, Christ revealing God to us and through us to the world.

Chapter 7

Jesus Christ, The Pattern

In the fifteenth chapter of John, Jesus related to His disciples the relationship between the vine and the branches. We will first back up to the Old Testament and note that Israel was a vine brought forth out of Egypt, which God planted and which took deep root (Ps. 80:8-9 KJV). Even though of pure seed (Jer. 2:21 Amp.), they brought forth wild grapes (Isa. 5:4 KJV). Jesus Christ is the **true** vine. *"I am the True Vine and My Father is the Vinedresser. Any branch in Me that does not bear fruit - that stops bearing - He cuts away (trims off, takes away). Dwell in Me and I will dwell in you - Live in Me and I will live in you. Just as **no branch can bear fruit of itself without abiding in** (vitally united to) **the vine,** neither can you bear fruit unless you abide in Me. I am the Vine, you are the branches. Whosoever lives in Me and I in him bears much (abundant) fruit. However, apart from Me - cut off from vital union with Me - you can do nothing. If a person does not dwell in Me, he is thrown out as a [broken-off] branch and withers. Such branches are gathered up and thrown out into the fire and they are burned. When you bear (produce) much fruit, My Father* *is honored and glorified; and you show and prove yourselves to be true followers of Mine"* (Jn. 15:1-2; 4-6; 8 Amp.).

He is the True Vine and we are the branches. Yet the branches that are alive to bear fruit are alive because Christ lives within them. They have to stay connected. It is a spiritual union between the vine and the branches. The fruit also contains the seed for the next generation and Christ is that Seed. That life that we then bring to others will also result in the manifestation of Jesus Christ within them.

Ezek. 43:10 KJV, "Thou son of man, show the house (the spiritual house of Jesus) to the house of Israel, (the carnal house of the house of Moses) that they may be ashamed of their iniquities: and let them measure the pattern." The Pattern is Jesus, walking in the Father's will and working the works of God.

The main purpose of Jesus coming to earth was to reveal the Father. Jesus Christ is not just an imitation but the express image of God. *"He is the sole expression of the glory of God - the Light-being, the out-raying of the divine - and He is the perfect imprint and very image of [God's] nature, upholding and maintaining and guiding and propelling the universe by His mighty word of power. When He had by offering Himself accomplished our cleansing of sin and riddance of guilt, He sat down at the right hand of the divine Majesty on high, [Taking a place and rank by which] He himself became as much superior to angels as the glorious Name (title) which He has inherited is different from and more excellent than theirs"* (He. 1:3-4 Amp.),

The word "image" used here comes from the Greek *charakter* showing the Son is both personally distant from, yet literally equal to God. He is the image of God's substance or essence. *"Who being in the form of God, thought it not robbery to be equal with God"* (Ph. 2:6).

Col. 1:15 Amp. reads: *"[Now] He is the exact likeness of the unseen God - **the visible representation of the invisible;** He is the Firstborn - of all creation."* God, through Jesus, became visible to both the natural eye and the spiritual eye. Earthly man could now see and perceive the very nature and character of God from the standpoint of their everyday life. Today, the Gospel accounts of the life of Jesus, as He revealed the invisible God, becomes visible to our spiritual eyes.

What was the mission of Jesus on the earth? How was He sustained? Let us examine a few Scriptures. *"My meat is to do the will of him that sent me, and to finish his work"* (Jn. 4:34 KJV). *"For the son of Man is come to save that which was lost"* (Mt. 18:11; Jn. 3:17). All mankind has been lost since the fall of Adam. *"Even as the Son of Man came not to be ministered unto but to minister, and to give his life a ransom for many"* (Mt. 20:28 KJV). He came to preach the kingdom of God (Lu. 4:43) and to send fire on the earth (Lu. 12:49). He came to be King and witness unto the truth (Jn. 18:37).

And in Lu. 4:18-19 KJV we read, *"The Spirit of the Lord is upon me to preach the gospel to the poor; he hath sent me to heal the brokenhearted, to preach deliverance to the captives, and recovering sight to the blind, to set at liberty them that are bruised, to preach the acceptable year of the Lord."*

It was part of the nature of Jesus to serve. He never ceased to serve and He serves even this day in our hearts. Phil. 2:7 KJV, *"But made himself of no reputation, and*

49

took upon him the form of a servant, and was made in the likeness of men:" In the gospel of John we read the account of Jesus washing the feet of His disciples. He voluntarily stripped Himself of His outer garments. Garments speak of a person's rank or position. He then girded Himself with a towel (Jn. 13:5), the symbol of the lowest ranking household servant of that culture. He then proceeded to wash their feet. So many Christians think they have graduated from being a servant. They would never stop to pick up a piece of trash on the floor of the church. That's beneath them. If He is the Pattern, then we, too, to manifest the nature of Jesus, must become servants of others.

Go to the Father

Jesus said, *"..because I go unto My Father"* (Jn. 14:12 KJV). Where is the Father? Not out in the sky somewhere or on another planet but the Bible states that God is Spirit (Jn. 4:24 NKJV). Jesus came from God, the spirit realm and manifested Himself among men in the soul realm. He had dominion over the soul realm (men's minds) and dominion over the plant and animal kingdom. Jesus told Pilate, *"...you would have no authority over me unless it had been given you from above..."* (Jn. 19:11 NAS).

Yet Jesus did not cease His work when He left the earth realm. What is to be accomplished in this age and the eons to come will be accomplished through a many membered Christ, the ascended Christ, indwelling and working in and through His saints (Jn. 14:20; Col. 2:19; 1 Co. 12:27).

Before the advent of Jesus Christ, God was considered as distant, out in the sky somewhere, impersonal, one to be afraid of, a God of condemnation, wrath and judgment, a

God without mercy. This concept was true, not only of the nation of Israel, but the heathen nations as well. Even today, many Christians are afraid of God, afraid He will pounce on them at the slightest mistake in their lives. To call God Father was blasphemous, yet Jesus called Him "Abba Father." We too, can call Him Abba Father (Ro. 8:15). The closest we can come to this in our western culture is to call our natural fathers "Daddy".

The "Abba" speaks not of a name but a relationship of the Son to the Father. To say "Abba" is to utter the closest word of love and kinship. Likewise, the term "Daddy" is not a name but a relationship to our natural father. My sisters and I called my father "Dad," but our daughter, who was born in 1952, has always called me "Daddy." Spiritually speaking, we should willingly and anxiously be able to crawl up on the lap of God and call Him "Abba." or "Daddy."

The Concordant Literal N.T. states in Col. 2:9, *"For in Him the entire complement of the Deity is dwelling bodily."* The Amplified: *"For in Him the whole fullness of Deity (the Godhead), continues to dwell in bodily form - giving complete expression of the divine nature."*

The word "bodily" is from Strong's #4985, *somatikos,* so-mat-ee-koce'; adv. from #4984; corporeally or physically - bodily. The word "dwelleth" (KJV) comes from *katoikeo,* from *kata,* down and *oikeo,* to dwell, meaning a permanent dwelling place. Continuing in v. 10 Amp., *"And you are in Him, made full and have come to fullness of life - in Christ you too are filled with the Godhead: Father, Son and Holy Spirit, and reach full Spiritual stature. And He is the Head of all rule and authority - of every angelic principality and power."*

Thus, if the divine nature of God, the fullness of the Deity dwells in Christ, and Christ dwells in us, then the Godhead dwells in us, in bodily form, **allowing His divine nature to manifest itself in and through our body**. In Jn. 17:5 Amp. Jesus prayed, *"And now Father, glorify Me along with Yourself and restore Me to such majesty and honor in Your presence as I had with you before the world existed."* Jesus became poor that we might be rich (2 Co. 8:9). How did He become poor? By giving up the glory He had with the Father. Now in this prayer, He asks to be restored to that glory.

We must back off and take a look at the whole. Here is the omniscient, omnipresent, omnipotent, awesome, mysterious God, the creator of the universe, a God that much of the world sees as unknowable, unreachable, impersonal. Yet this same God demonstrated to the world the total possibility, through His Son Jesus Christ, that His (God's) nature and character, even the invisible God, could be manifested in visible form in terms that the common man could see, perceive, feel, experience, discern, appreciate, understand, and relate to in his everyday life. What's more, that same nature and character, through the indwelling Jesus Christ, can now manifest in and through man. Jesus told Philip, If you have seen me, you have seen the Father.

Chapter 8

The Person of Jesus Christ

In Acts 15:14 KJV we read, *"Simeon hath declared how God at the first did visit the Gentiles, to take out of them a people for his name. "* These people are the Sons of God which become His name personified. Here "name" means nature, attributes, character and image.

God demonstrated first through the Person of Jesus Christ that His (God's) image and likeness, His very nature could be manifested in human form, one who would do only the will of the Father. Even though Jesus appeared as a man on the earth, He manifested the divine nature of God in the confines of a finite human body and in the environment of the earth, in the midst of and in contact with fallen man. This also is a pattern for the sons of God to follow.

"If ye had known me, ye should have known my Father also, and from henceforth ye know him and have seen him" (Jn. 14:7 KJV). And in Jn. 12:45 KJV we read, *"And he that seeth me seeth him that sent me. "* Jesus was not saying that if you have seen my physical appearance, my facial features, that you have seen the Father. Multitudes had seen Jesus' physical appearance, even listened to His

teaching and had seen Him perform miracles. But few saw Him with their spiritual eyes, to see that He was actually the son of God, that He was the express image of God, not a physical likeness, for God is spirit. He was saying that if you've seen my character, my nature, they are identical with the Father's.

The Humanity of Jesus

Jesus was born as a baby like all mankind, coming from the heavenly, invisible realm of the Father, entering this physical, natural, visible world. He grew into manhood like an ordinary person, except that He knew who He was. He ate, slept, became tired, walked, and wept, just like an ordinary human being, as any other person, in the limits of time and space. Except for a few times of miraculous power, He voluntarily limited Himself to the natural laws of the earth.

Can we learn anything of the attributes and divine nature of God by knowing His Son Jesus Christ, by knowing Him as a person, qualities that could be ascribed to a human, a personal human being, (a spiritual man) as opposed to angels or other living creatures? Yes, we can.

He. 4:15 KJV, *"For we have not an high priest which cannot be touched with the feeling of our infirmities; but was in all points tempted like as we are, yet without sin."* Ro. 8:3 KJV, *"For what the law could not do, in that it was weak through the flesh, God sending his own Son in the likeness of sinful flesh, and for sin, condemned sin in the flesh:"*

Jesus appeared to others as an ordinary man. (Isa. 53:2). Yet He was unique in certain ways. First of all, Jesus had a unique birth. He was with God and was God (Jn. 1:10), becoming flesh (Jn. 1:14). He was conceived by the Holy Spirit, born of a virgin. Jesus was unique in His life, a life without sin. He acted and spoke apart from sin (1 Jn. 3:5; 1 Pe. 2:22). He spoke nothing but the words of spirit and life; He spoke as one with authority. He was always in the Father's will. He performed miracles. He declared, *"If I had not done among them the **works which none other man did,** they had not sin..."* (Jn. 15:24 KJV). Likewise, those sons of God who are filled with the spirit and have His life indwelling in them will do the same things and be the same way as Jesus is.

The death of Jesus was unique. His death was not that of a simple martyr or like other prophets before or after Him . His suffering in the garden tells us of the weight of the sinful world upon His very being. He hung on the cross, not as others but as a man who knew no sin, and was made an offering for sin that we might be made the righteousness of God in Him (2 Co. 5:24). Death on the cross was one of the most cruel forms of death devised by carnal man, yet God chose the cross for the sacrifice of His only begotten Son. It was this sacrifice that opened the Holy of Holies so that the sons of God could enter.

Jesus was unique in His resurrection. Without the resurrection, all hope of Christianity fades to nothing. Over 500 people witnessed the resurrected Christ. The truth of the resurrected Christ is the foundation which brings reality to all other aspects of the Person and the work of Jesus Christ. The resurrection is a historical fact but more importantly, the indwelling, living Christ in the hearts of millions for almost 2000 years, including millions today, attest to the spiritual reality, the eternal.

No other prophet of history can boast of an empty tomb. No other religion of the world can boast of a leader risen from the grave and alive today, alive by His spirit in the hearts of mankind.

Life Abundantly

Those who believe on the Person of Jesus Christ and His resurrection have experienced **the regenerating touch of God** in their lives. Jesus said, *"I came that they might have life (ZOE- spiritual life) and that they might have it more abundantly"* (Jn. 10:10 KJV). In one's initial salvation experience, God presents to that person, not a doctrine, not a revelation (apart from Jesus Christ), not a set of laws to obey, not a teaching, not a plan of life, but He presents a Person, Jesus Christ, for His Spirit is joined to the believer's spirit, making them one new entity.

*"Let this same attitude and purpose and [humble] mind be in you which was in Christ Jesus - Let Him be your example in humility - Who, although being essentially one with God and in the form of God **[possessing the fullness of the attributes which make God God]** did not think this equality with God was a thing to be eagerly grasped or retained; but stripped Himself [of all privileges and rightful dignity] as to assume the guise of a servant (slave) **in that He became like men and was born a human being**, and after He had appeared in human form He abased and humbled Himself [still further] and carried His obedience to the extreme of death, even death of (the) cross! Therefore [because He stooped so low], God has highly exalted Him and has freely bestowed on Him the name that is above every name"* (Phil. 2:5-9 Amp.).

"And he that seeth me seeth him that sent me" (Jn. 12:45 KJV). *"But now I go my way to him that sent me; and none of you asketh me, Whither goest thou?"* (Jn. 16:5 KJV). Jesus had stepped out of the invisible realm of the heaven (with the Father) and stepped into the visible realm of man, that is, man on earth. Much of what He demonstrated in way of acts and miracles on the earth plane were but a pattern or a shadow for the many membered sons and the kingdom age. For example, His healing of the lame was but a shadow of the healing of the spiritual walk of men in the kingdom age. And the healing of the blind represents the healing of spiritual blindness of people in the kingdom age. Therefore as He is, so are we in this life.

Jesus then stepped back into the invisible realm (back to the Father) but returned via the Holy Spirit or His own Spirit to indwell in men on the earth. *"These things have I spoken unto you being yet present with you. But the Comforter, which is the Holy Ghost, whom the Father will send in my name (nature), he will teach you all things, and bring all things to your remembrance, whatsoever I have said unto you"* (Jn. 14:25-26 KJV). (See also Jn. 17:11, 13; Jn. 16:7, 16).

For beginning on the day of Pentecost, Jesus Christ, Who, possessing the nature, the attributes, the very life of God, dwelt within man and began to manifest Himself within man and began one by one to transform the nature of man. Witness the tremendous transformation of the nature of Peter and the other disciples after Pentecost. Likewise, notice the change in the Apostle Paul after his Damascus experience. Now it is our turn.

This manifestation (of the nature of Jesus Christ) in the personhood of mankind began first and is now developing in a firstfruit company. They too are to become perfected, come into the image of God, bearing life and light to the rest of the world. (Mt. 5:48; Eph. 4:12).

"Be not conformed to this world, but be ye transformed (metamorphoo) by the renewing of your mind" (Ro. 12:2 KJV). The Greek here again suggests an entirely new creation, a creation possessing the very nature and attributes of God, the same as manifested in the Person of Jesus Christ as brought out in the Scriptures: life, meekness, patience, love, love of the Father, temperance, godliness, holiness, humbleness, compassion, etc.

In 1 Co. 11:7 KJV we read, *"For a man indeed ought not to cover his head, forasmuch as he is **the image and glory of God**..."* Here in the case of man, the word "image" refers to "man as he was created, being a visible representation of God, a being corresponding to the original" - W.E. Vine

How Do We Acquire
the Attributes of Jesus Christ?

How do we acquire the attributes of Jesus Christ, His meekness, humility, love, patience, purity etc., that we are discussing? Eph. 4:15 states, *"But speaking the truth in love, may **grow up into Him**, in all things which is the head, even Christ."* Amp.: *"Grow up in every way and in all things into Him."*

The number five in the bible stands for grace and also for the five fold ministry. In Ep. 4:10-12 NKJV we read, Eph 4:10 *"He who descended is also the One who ascended far above all the heavens, that He might fill all things.) And He Himself gave some to be apostles, some prophets, some evangelists, and some pastors and teachers, for the equipping of the saints for the work of ministry, for the edifying of the body of Christ."*

Reading further from the Amplified, v. 13, *"[That it might develop] until we all attain oneness in the faith and in the comprehension of the full and accurate knowledge of the Son of God; that [we might arrive] at really mature manhood - **the completeness of personality** which is nothing less than the standard height of Christ's own perfection - the measure of the stature of the fullness of the Christ, and the completeness found in Him."*

The Scriptures clearly point out that the change of man into the image of God involves a process. We do not awake some morning and suddenly find ourselves transformed into His image or into a fully manifested son of God. We grow up into the Head, which is Christ. This Head is the ascension ministry or a five fold order called the five fold ministry.

The Veil Is Rent

We read 2 Co. 3:16-17 NAS: *"But whenever a man turns (Amp.: in repentance) to the Lord, the veil is taken away. Now the Lord is the Spirit, and where the Spirit of the lord is, there is liberty."* Amplified (v. 18): *"And all of us, as with unveiled face, [because we] continued to behold [in the word of God] as in a mirror the glory of the Lord, are **constantly being transfigured** into His very own image in ever increasing splendor and from one degree of glory to another [for this comes] from the lord [Who is] the Spirit."*

The verb "transfigured" (*metamorphoo* or as a

caterpillar to a butterfly) is first person plural (we), present indicative (taking place continually - Amp.: "constantly"). The tense indicates a process, a process whereby we are being brought into perfection through time - toward the fullness of the nature of Christ. It is in the passive voice (being done to us), that is, by the Spirit of the Lord.

The veil has been rent, the way opened into the realm of God, the Father. *"Having therefore, brethren, boldness to enter into the Holiest by the blood of Jesus **by a new and living way**, which He hath consecrated for us, through the veil, that is to say, His flesh"* (He. 10:19-20).

The Israelites would not accept Jesus Christ as their Lord because their faces were veiled with their traditional interpretation of the Scriptures (2 Co. 3:14-15). The image we are being changed into is that of Christ in all His moral excellencies. It's when you yield to His Lordship as ruler over every facet of your life that the veil of natural understanding is taken away and He transforms you. You turn to Jesus not just as Saviour or Baptizer but to Him as Lord.

To progress in the Lord, and in order to come into His image and His likeness, we need to grow spiritually. We must not shrink back from the deeper, stronger teachings of the Scriptures. He. 5:14 (RSV) states, *"But solid food is for the mature, for those who have their faculties trained by practice to distinguish good from evil."*

John the Baptist declared, *"He must increase, I must decrease"* (Jn. 3:30). We must not only do the same, that is, increase the nature of Christ within us, but walk out the reality of that day by day. We are not robots for Christ who would take over our entire being. But as we progressively submit our will to His will, the two become one will. *"That they all may be one; as thou Father, art in me, and I in thee, that they also may be one in us: that the world may believe that thou hast sent me"* (Jn. 17:21).

One of the most important attributes of God is that He produces life, that is, Zoe, or spiritual life. Jesus Christ manifested that life while on the earth and continues to manifest it more so via the Holy Spirit in man, Christ in you. That life that man receives is not something man is supposed to grasp for himself, that is, use God's blessings (and the Seed of Christ) only for his own enjoyment. But man, that is, initially the firstfruits company, **in turn, who have the power of the indwelling person of Jesus Christ, are to bring life to the earth plane,** to a dying and sick world, even to the hostile environment and in the midst of the enemies of God (Ro. 5:10; Eph. 2:12) and to all creation. Put another way, if Jesus Christ is our Pattern, and He is, and He cast His seed into the earth, that is, into man, then the sonship company of man likewise is to cast the Seed of Christ from within them into the earth, this time, to the rest of creation who are groaning for the manifestation of the sons of God.

That man is to partake of the divine nature of God is seen from the Scriptures: 2 Pet 1:3-8, *"According as his divine power hath given unto us all things that pertain unto life and godliness, through the knowledge of him that hath called us to glory and virtue: Whereby are given unto us exceeding great and precious promises: that by these ye might be partakers of the divine nature, having escaped the corruption that is in the world through lust. And beside this, giving all diligence, add to your faith virtue ...knowledge...temperance...patience... godliness...brotherly kindness...charity. For if these things be in you, and abound, they make you that ye shall neither be barren nor unfruitful in the knowledge of our Lord Jesus Christ."*

The word "partake" comes from the Greek *koinunus*, an adjective used as a noun, denoting a companion, partner, partaker (Vine). We don't have to wait until some distant future to be a partaker of His divine nature. We have it now. We can not only know, enjoy and experience God's love, mercy, patience etc. but we can demonstrate these same natures to others,

We can experience the peace of God in the midst of our trials but we can also bring the reality of this same divine peace to the turmoil of others, whether it be one on one or a group of people. We can not only know and experience God's forgiveness for us, but can forgive others with the same divine nature. Furthermore, we can love the unlovable.

Chapter 9

The Seed of Christ

John 12:24 (KJV), *"Verily, verily, I say unto you, Except a corn of wheat fall into the ground and die, it abideth alone: but if it die, it bringeth forth much fruit."* This verse brings in much of the principles of the Kingdom of God. Using the parallel of a natural seed, Jesus was speaking of Himself. Two conditions had to be met. First, it must fall to the earth AND secondly, it must die. He had to fall to the earth, that is, **fall** or descend from the heavenly realm to a lesser realm, the earth realm. He also had to die to His earthly identity just as a natural seed must die to its identity. If He continued to dwell as Jesus of Nazareth, He would abide alone as the only spirit filled person in the earth. It is also implied that the fruit contains the seed for the next generation. There would be a viable, life generating seed within that fruit.

Jesus is the one who plants His seed, Himself, into mankind, the earth. Demonstrated here (Jn. 12:24), are not only death, burial and resurrection, but also growth, maturity, and the production of seed, - it is destined to grow, it is destined to bear fruit, and it is destined to reproduce, after its parent, after its own kind, whether plant, animal, or the life of Jesus Christ. Gen. 1:11 (KJV), *"And God said, Let the earth bring forth grass, the herb yielding seed, and the fruit tree yielding fruit after his kind, whose seed is in itself, upon the earth: and it was so."* NAS: *"...with seed in them..."* NIV: *"...bear fruit with seed in it...".*

Gen. 1:24 NKJV, "Then God said, *"Let the earth bring forth the living creature according to its kind: cattle and creeping thing and beast of the earth, each according to its kind";* and it was so."* NIV: *"...each according to its kind..."* **This is Christ in you** (Col. 1:27). The Hebrew for "kind" is *miyn* or species, thus, each according to its own species.

The Soil Needs the Seed

The soil needs the seed and the seed needs the soil. The soil has no life in itself and will produce nothing until a seed is planted in it. Without the seed it remains dead or lifeless. It cannot produce any higher form of life than itself. Yet the seed needs a medium, the soil, in which to plant itself. No matter how perfect a seed is, even if it has a potential of one hundred percent germination, unless it is planted, it remains alone and cannot produce a harvest.

As the soil needs the seed, so the Adamic race needs the seed of Christ. And as the seed needs the soil, so Christ, the Seed, needs a medium in which to plant Himself. The dirt of a field is not harvested, but left in the field. So the dust or "earthy" of man is not harvested. God is not interested in a washed "dirt", nor a reformed Adam. He is after that which is produced out of that Adamic earthy man by the Seed that was planted in it. Flesh and blood, that is, the

Adamic nature, shall never inherit the kingdom of God.

Phil. 3:21 NAS, *"Who (the Lord Jesus Christ) will transform the body of our humble state into conformity with the body of His glory, by the exertion of the power that He has even to subject all things to Himself."* But He cannot do this except by the man of the earth. The Head of the body needs the rest of the body (1 Co. 12:21). God is bringing forth a people who possess His divine nature, a nature produced from that divine Seed within them.

Fall into the Earth and Die

The natural seed falls **into** (not on top of) the ground and subjects itself to what we will call the law of the soil, that is, the temperature, moisture, atmospheric pressure, soil structure and the seasons. In a like manner, Jesus, even though He was in heaven while on earth (Jn. 3:13), as the Seed, He fell into the depths of the earth and voluntarily subjected Himself to the law of the earth. That is, He subjected Himself to not only civil law, but to a finite body, to the dimensions of time and space, to day and night, to hunger, even to the culture of His time. And yes, He rubbed shoulders with sinful man. At His trial He opened not His mouth, but subjected Himself to the whims of those accusing Him and to those who would hang Him on the cross.

Here is the depth of the earth in which the Seed, Jesus was planted - the depth of sin of mankind. That Seed had to be planted deep into the earth. There is no person on the face of the earth, past, present or future, who is so deep in sin that God cannot or will not save. That incorruptible Seed planted in the worst sinner will take root and grow and raise that person to life. That is a kingdom principle. The Jews thought it all right to hang an innocent man on the cross but they made sure he was down before the Sabbath (Jn. 19:31). Oh, the depth of hypocrisy and depth of the sin of mankind, the depth of the earth where Jesus was planted.

Except for the outer shell, which dies, the natural seed (really its embryo), does not become a part of that soil but arises from that soil to new life. So Jesus, living amid the earthen realm (man), and the law of sin and death, did not become a part of that earth but rose to new life. Likewise the body of Christ - as it follows the pattern of Jesus, does not become a part of the law of sin and death, but arises from it. When we are born again, we are no longer humans but spirit beings, no longer of that earth realm (Jn. 17:14). As for the natural seed, the embryo does not become a part of the soil, even though it eventually draws nutrients from it.

Man also subjects himself to the death of the outer man or shell so that the life of Jesus can come forth to manifest His nature. If God is to manifest His nature through the sons of God, then we must have a burden for the lost, even those deep in sin. We must fully recognize the love that God has for the world.

We must state a law relative to our discussions, a law of the hierarchy among God's creations. The soil cannot raise itself up into the plant kingdom, those of the plant kingdom cannot raise themselves up into the animal kingdom, the animals cannot raise themselves into the kingdom of the natural man, and the natural man cannot raise himself into the kingdom of God, the spiritual kingdom. Instead, he must be born into it (Jn.3:3).

Just as a natural seed springs forth in the earth in which it is planted, so Christ Jesus springs forth in the earth realm, that is, in man. This began on the day of Pentecost. It's a universal law. The life within the embryo of a seed must spring forth when planted in good ground (Gen. 1:11; Mk. 4:20)

In order for Jesus the Christ to come to the earth (seed falling to the ground), He had to appear, function and die as a man. Yet He was not only all Man but all God. Jesus had to lay down His life, plant it in the earth so that Seed could germinate. New life must come forth. With Him, it was resurrection life. Where is that resurrection life manifested? In the spiritual, invisible realm? No! In the earth realm - in earthen vessels - in you and me. A natural seed springs forth out of the earth or ground - out of that realm just below the realm of the parent plant. In like manner, that new life originated from the Seed, the seed of the spiritual Christ, but it now rises from the natural man, that realm just below the parent, and **manifests** itself in the earthly man to bring (spiritual) life to him, first through the new birth. (Jn. 3:3), then the Pentecostal experience (Ac. 1:8). Then that same life goes forth **from** the spirit filled person to bring life to the world.

Abide Alone

The disciples did not understand Jesus. He was still alone - outside of them. That transforming power was not yet working in them. But after Pentecost, notice the change in Peter. Jesus was no longer alone for His Spirit had multiplied and now dwelt within Peter and the others - the 120 in the upper room..

What if Jesus had not died on calvary, but had lived until now, never aging, always living in a 33 year old body, teaching the Kingdom and performing miracles among the people of the world. He would still abide alone.

Unless Jesus died, He would be the single, solitary individual on the face to the earth to possess eternal life, the only one Who could legitimately manifest the nature of God. He would be the only one to communicate by the Spirit with God, the only one to speak words of life, the only one to possess immortality. He would be a head without a body. The manifestation of the Sons of God could not even begin to materialize.

The manifestation of God in the earth was first limited to one finite being, Jesus of Nazareth. When He died, His seed was planted in the earth and rose again - His life would then become manifested in a many membered body and eventually to the world. His mission was not to abide alone or remain on the cross, but to produce much fruit.

Jesus, Who came from the heavenly realm, was as Joseph, a stranger in a strange land, dwelling in the earth realm. His own received Him not. Jesus at Gethsemane prayed alone. All but Peter and John fled from Him at His trial and John would not speak up at the trial to save Him. John was the only disciple at the cross.

What about after the cross and His resurrection? From the verse *"...every eye shall see Him"* (Re. 1:7 KJV), some people believe that this means "at His so called second coming, Jesus will appear on worldwide TV." Let me assure you, even if that would happen, as far as the unconverted are concerned, He would still abide alone, for His seed would not have been planted in their earth (body) to produce new life.

As for the saved, His physical appearance would not, as is commonly taught, suddenly bring them into perfection, or into some type of manifestation.

Let us add, if you are looking for a physical man who looks like Jesus of Nazareth did, you will be disappointed. He appeared in a different "form" to Mary at the tomb (Jn. 20:14), to the men on the road to Emmaus (Lu. 24:13-15) and even to His disciples on the shores of Galilee (Jn. 21:4). From Mk. 16:12, *"After that he appeared in another form unto two of them, as they walked, and went into the country."* Jesus can appear in many forms to us today.

The teaching or even His works basically was not what was to be multiplied, though that would be a by-product. (We are to do greater works. Jn. 14:12). What was to be multiplied was Himself, His person, His divine nature, via His Seed planted in mankind. God sent His Son (the *Seed*) to the earth, not to abide alone but to die that He be planted in man to bring forth that life, His very image. Jesus was to multiply Himself in man and each new generation of enchristed ones also multiply the Christ in others.

Much Fruit

What is the fruit? W. E. Vine states: "...fruit being the visible expression of power working inwardly and invisibly, the character of the fruit being evidence of the character of the power producing it (Mt. 7:16). As the visible expression of hidden lusts are the works of the flesh, so the invisible power of the Holy Spirit in those who are brought into living union with Christ (Jn. 15:2-8, 16) produces the fruit of the Spirit (Ga. 5:22), the singular form suggesting the unity of the character of the Lord as reproduced in them, namely, *"love, joy, peace, longsuffering, kindness, goodness, faithfulness, meekness, temperance..."*

Bearing fruit and coming into maturity is not allocated to the distant future or to the other side of the grave. That would not follow God's order for total growth. Neither is the fruit we bear likened to some shriveled up, scabby, deformed or unripe apple. But because it bears the pure seed of Christ within, it is a purely formed fruit.

The fruit of a Christian is not saving souls, (for souls just won are but babes), preaching, evangelizing, singing hymns, or writing messages or books...**The fruit is the manifestation of the character and nature of Jesus Christ who resides within.** Jesus said, *"you shall know them by their fruit"* (Mt. 7:20).

A tree is identified by its fruit. Do men gather grapes of thorns, or figs of thistles? (Mt. 7:16 KJV). *"A good tree cannot bring forth evil fruit, neither can a corrupt tree bring forth good fruit"* (Mt. 7:18 KJV). Why is an apple tree called an apple tree? Not because of its bark, its leaves or its shape, but because it bears apples. Read this with spiritual eyes. The apples it bears or the character of those apples is the manifestation of the invisible character and power within the tree. When you bite into an apple, you don't expect it to taste like a peach. It tastes like an apple, looks like an apple, cooks like an apple, has all the nutritive value of an apple, it even keeps like an apple. Equally important, it bears the seed for the next generation of apples, even that same variety. Likewise with a Christian. Within that Christian is not only the nature of Christ to be manifested, but the pure seed of Christ for the next generation of believers.

So the fruit you bear - the fruit from the seed of Christ within, has all the characteristics of the Christ. It is not contaminated with the Adam nature; it manifests itself , "tastes like", looks like it's the Christ, because it is. When people "bite into it", that is, partake of it, consume it, have contact with it, it will be the Christ. When a person witnesses to a lost soul, the saving grace of Jesus Christ and that seed takes root. It will not be a mixture; it will be the Christ that grows and manifests itself in that person. **A seed can produce only what it is**.

We ask the question, "From where did that Seed, Jesus of Nazareth, come?" Who did the people think He was? *"And they (the Jews) said, Is not this Jesus, the son of Joseph, whose father and mother we know? How is it then that he saith, I came down from heaven?"* (Jn. 6:42 KJV). Herod thought He was John the Baptist raised from the dead (Mt. 14:2). He was called a *prophet* (Jn. 4:19), and a *teacher* (Jn. 3:2). Some of the Jews thought He was a *Samaritan* (Jn. 8:48). The man healed of blindness first spoke of Him as *a man* called Jesus (Jn. 9:11).

We read in Jn. 8:42, *"Jesus said unto them (Jews), If God were your father, you would love me;* ***for I proceeded forth and came from God*** *and neither came I of myself, but He sent Me."* In Jn. 8:14 (Wuest Translation) Jesus spoke, *"..Even If I am bearing testimony, concerning myself, my testimony is true, because I know with an absolute knowledge from where I came and where I am departing."* Verse 18 (KJV): *"I am one that bears witness of myself and* ***the Father that sent me*** *beareth witness of me."*

Jesus was God. *"In the beginning was the Word and the Word was with God, and the Word was God"* (Jn. 1:1

KJV). And in Jn. 10:30 KJV, *"I and my Father are one."*
Wuest Translation: *"I and the Father are one in essence."*
Jesus spoke to the Jews: *"..you are from beneath, I am
from above; ye are of this world, I am not of this world. I
said therefore unto you, that ye shall die in your sins; for
if ye believe not that I am he, ye shall die in your sins"* (Jn.
8:23-24).

As a plant matures, it begins to develop its fruit which
also contains the seed for the next generation - so the sons
of God - as they mature, manifest the fruit - you know a
tree by its fruit.- joy, peace, etc. Fruit is not meant to be
just consumed in "one generation" but the seed in that fruit
contains life and is to be planted into the next "generation."

It's a universal law - seed produces after its own kind.
If you sow wheat, you'll get wheat, which in turn will
produce more wheat which carries the germ of the wheat.
If you plant corn, you'll get not only corn but with the
inherited characteristics of a particular variety. The seed of
Adam produces nothing but death and the adamic nature,
whereas the seed of Christ produces nothing but life. The
seed of Christ planted in the earth (mankind) can produce
only one thing - a Christ like nature and character, in its
maturity. The Christ seed in you will not - it cannot - it
never will - produce - nor manifest, anything other than the
Christ nature.

Just as a natural seed of a plant or animal carries not
only the identical DNA for the following generations, it
also carries the potential embryo and continuous life. So
likewise the seed of Christ contains all the necessary
"ingredients" to manifest the image and likeness, the very
life (Zoe or spiritual life) of Jesus Christ - but also contains
the embryo that can be passed on to the next generation of

72

believers; and the next, etc.

You may say, I can show anger, lose patience, etc. once in a while. Your soul is yet to be saved. Neither will that Christ nature cause you to manifest anything else but that divine nature. That other nature comes from the soul (mind, will and emotions) which is still in the process of being saved (Ro.12:2). Salvation of the soul is progressive. God will not cause you to sin.

When the sons of God or any believer witnesses to a lost soul, so that they are born again (Jn. 3:3 KJV), that seed of Christ is a pure seed, even though the person may have mixed some natural words with the spiritual words. If the spiritual words, the life, fall into that ground, planted into that person, (if you will) it will produce a pure Jesus Christ nature, (spirit saved) - no mixture. It will eventually mature and manifest itself as the nature of Jesus Christ.

The seed of Christ has never has been contaminated, is not now contaminated in the hearts of believers, and never can be contaminated. It will be a pure incorruptible seed for generations to come, into eternity.

Just as the soil and moisture of the ground as a lower realm cannot become part of the plant, except as nutrients within the plant, so nothing of the lower nature of man can become or inherit the kingdom of God.

What do we see regarding the death and burial and resurrection of Jesus - the seed falling to the earth to die? Do we believe with spiritual understanding that our old man was (past tense) crucified with Him (Ro. 6:6). Do we believe we were reconciled to God by His death? (Ro. 5:10). Do we believe we are buried with Him? (Ro. 6:4). Then are we living and walking out what we believe? Do we believe in all the scriptural truths regarding the resurrection? Do we believe that same resurrection power that raised Jesus from the earth now works in us? Do we recognize or discern the power of the resurrection in our daily life - to see and understand spiritually - to see Him in His purpose, His mission - to fall to the earth, to die, to come to life and bear much fruit - to see that the nature of Jesus Christ is that of His Father from where He came and that divine nature is to be manifested in a many membered body **now**, not just in the distant future?

First the natural , then the spiritual. Think first of natural fruit, vegetable, grains, trees etc. Then the spiritual - produce after their own kind.

Paths to Follow

Leaders of the past have blazed a trail for us to follow. They include the Apostle Paul, Martin Luther, John Calvin, John Wesley, Smith Wigglesworth, George Hawtin, B.S. Westlake, Daniel W. Willhite, and Bill Britton. Not only have these leaders tread a path for us to follow but so have dedicated saints, those filled with the Holy Spirit, who lived a life of holiness, who pressed on with God. These leaders have passed on to the other side, but they would not want us to stop where they left off; rather that we, too, press on in God to greater heights that they would have dreamed of.

If a teacher really teaches, the student should surpass the teacher in wisdom and knowledge by a significant degree. That is the manifestation of the Sons of God, that many sons might be brought unto glory, even a greater and greater glory. We are changed from glory to glory.

2 Cor 3:18 KJV, *"But we all, with open face beholding*

as in a glass the glory of the Lord, are changed into the same image from glory to glory, even as by the Spirit of the Lord."

Chapter 10

The Role of Man

God did not intend for man to continually walk in despair and defeat; neither continually walk in the fallen adamic nature nor in the realm of death. Man was created to live, not die (Ro. 5:17, 18, 21; 6:4, 8, 11). Isa. 60:1-2 KJV reads: *"**Arise (from the depression and prostration in which circumstances have kept you: rise to a new life)! Shine** - be radiant with the glory of the Lord; for your light is come, and the glory of the Lord is risen upon you! For behold, darkness shall cover the earth, and dense darkness all peoples; but the Lord shall arise upon you. (O, Jerusalem) and His glory shall be seen on you."*

The expression, "your light" means your happiness. "Your light **is** come" - present tense. Note that also the Lord does not come "down from heaven" as many think, but He arises within you from where He dwells.

In Hosea 5:15 - 6:1 KJV we read, *"I will go and return to my place, till they acknowledge their offense, and seek my face: in their affliction they will seek me early. Come and let us return unto the Lord: for he hath torn, and he will heal us; he hath smitten, and he will bind us up."* We will never see the face of God until we acknowledge our offense, that is, the ways of the flesh and of the carnal mind, the paths, if you will, of the sea (humanity) which live by the flesh and the carnal mind.

Ro. 12:2 KJV tells us, *"And be not conformed to this world* (age): *but be ye transformed by the renewing of your mind, that ye may prove what is that good* (30 fold) *and acceptable* (60 fold) *and perfect* (100 fold) *will of God."* From the Phillips translation: *"Don't let the world around you squeeze you into its own mold, but let God remold your minds from within, so that you may prove in practice that the plan of God for you is good, meets all his demands and moves toward the goal of true maturity."*

In other words, be not conformed to the world, the way it thinks, speaks and acts, the paths it follows. If we put death in, it will feed death to all parts of our body and we will die. But if we put life in it, it will feed life to all parts, even to every cell of our body and we will live.

A few more Scriptures that shed light on the role of man: Ps. 8:6 NKJV, *"You have made him (man) to have dominion over the works of Your hands; You have put all things under his feet,"* Ps. 82:6, KJV, *"I have said, Ye are gods; and all of you are children (sons) of the most High"* (El Elyon). And in Mt. 6:30, *"Wherefore, if God so clothe the grass of the field, which to day is, and tomorrow is cast into the oven, shall he not much more clothe you, O ye of little faith?"* This speaks of the spiritual clothing that God promises us.

We, the children of God, not those of the world, are the standard. The world's standard includes their philosophy of life, how they think and reason, what, how and why they do things. (Ps. 1:1-2) The world certainly tries to get us into their standard with the influence of its secular media and its secular life style. We have become the standard which the world should see or follow.

Our identity should be with Jesus, not with our Adamic nature and the problems we have in life. If we are to manifest the Christ, then we need to identify with the Christ who dwells within, rather than the flesh and its failures, negative thoughts etc. We have these problems because we identify with the flesh. Christ liveth in me, He is our identity. (2 Co. 6:16).

Before the earthly ministry of Jesus Christ, God spoke to man through His prophets and through His miracles, and primarily to only one group of people, the Israelites (He. 1:1). Then God demonstrated through the person of Jesus Christ, the Man, that the power, attributes and **the very nature of God could be manifested in the form of a man,** and that these same characteristics, through the power of the Holy Spirit, would reach even mortal man in the very life, even to the very depth of his thoughts.

Jesus then went one step further. He said it was expedient that He go away that the Comforter might come (Jn. 16:7). He came that the nature, power and attributes of God would more than dwell among men but that God Himself via the Holy Spirit would indwell man.

Vessels of Clay

We, mankind, were vessels made of clay, that is, of the earthly realm. As we empty ourselves (self) from that vessel, then Christ fills it with Himself. In the tabernacle in the wilderness, the altar was made of wood, representing humanity. In Ex. 30:3 KJV we read of the altar: *"Thou shalt overlay it with pure gold, the top thereof, and the sides thereof round about...*" Gold speaks of God or divinity, the perfect divine nature of God. Here, as a type, we see where God meets man - God so overshadowing (overlaying) man that man and his human nature is not seen. Man's individual personality, however, is not done away with.

Yet man, as that vessel, is essential as a means in which God may dwell in the earth, and in which to manifest His divine nature. God dwelt in the Most Holy Place of the tabernacle in the wilderness. Likewise, God's purpose is to permanently dwell in man, the living temple, one made without hands, made of lively stones. (Mk. 14:58; 1 Pe. 2:5).

When God "covers" man with His divine nature, the process begins by saving man's spirit, then his soul and eventually the body is redeemed. So God works from the inside out. As God works through that process, He becomes a greater and greater manifestation in and through man.

Jesus Christ, the Man, set the pattern for man. He manifested the nature of God, not by sitting on a physical throne in Herod's temple, but by living day by day within the confines and limitations of man (except sin and the sin nature) in an earthly body, but with the attributes and nature of God. He was all man and all God - the pattern for man (us) to follow.

Jesus Christ brought the nature and attributes of God, the very life of God into **human, visible form** (in the earth). Now with the empowering Jesus Christ within us, the sons of God can manifest that very nature to the world Jn. 17:21, "*That they all may be one; as thou, Father, art in me, and I in thee, that they also may be one in us: that* *the world may believe that thou hast sent me."* The sons do not manifest that nature by "trying to be Christlike," but by allowing the Lord Jesus Christ to manifest Himself through them.

God has purposed that there be a family of many membered sons to be just like His only begotten Son. He has a paternal desire to extend Himself to mankind, not just in nature and character but that His sons would do His bidding and His will in the earth.

Isaiah (53:2 KJV), speaking of Christ, said, *"...he hath no form or comeliness."* (Heb. "magnificence", i.e. ornament or splendor), which meant He looked like an ordinary man. God chose not angels, nor plants or animals nor wood or stone images, nor stars or any other of His creations but He chose **man** to manifest His nature. The first man to manifest that nature in the fullness was Jesus Christ, the only begotten Son of God.

Jesus spoke and acted nothing but Life - so the law of life, which is a higher law, superseded the law of sin and death which worked around Him. Man (the spiritual man), following Jesus as the pattern, as he speaks life from the (Holy) Spirit within him, thus also supersedes the law of sin and death (Ro. 8:2-6). How? By the power of God within (Jn. 17:21). It's the law of the Spirit of Life that enables man to live soberly and righteously in this present age.

Speaking of the essence of Christ becoming as a man, Paul wrote to the Philippians, *"Who being in the **form of God**, thought it not robbery to be equal with God,: but made Himself of no reputation, took upon him the **form of a servant**, and was made in the likeness of men"* (Phil. 2:6-7 KJV). The Concordant Literal N.T.: *"..who being* *inherently in the form of God...nevertheless empties Himself, taking the form of a slave, coming to be in the likeness of humanity."*

From the previous verse (5) (Amp.): *"Let this same attitude (inward) and purpose (outward) and [humble] mind (inward) be in you which was in Christ Jesus Let Him be your example in humility."* Thus, we go from inward to outward back to inward. It is when man humbles himself as Christ, The Pattern did, who divests himself of all authority, and takes on the attitude and mind of Christ, that man is then able to acquire what Christ was, the very nature of God. *"He who has found his life shall lose it, and he who has lost his life for my sake shall find it"* (Mt. 10:39 NAS).

We see from these verses that man is to advance from one experience to the next. As we receive spiritual wisdom and knowledge, come closer to God by hearing or reading the Word, by hearing a song, by walking out what Word we hear etc., rather than settle in one place, we should be able to move on to greater spiritual heights. God has given His Word to us in order to change our lives - change them into His image, not to satisfy our intellectual curiosity or to puff up our knowledge.

From Rev. 17:1 we read of the great harlot who sits on many waters. Now verse 5 from the same chapter NKJV, *"And on her forehead a name was written: MYSTERY, BABYLON THE GREAT, THE MOTHER OF HARLOTS AND OF THE ABOMINATIONS OF THE EARTH."* From the Scriptures, Babylon is a type of the corrupt political, economic, and religious systems which are a product of the carnal mind. Babylon will be destroyed (Re. 14:8; 18:2-4).

"And the land shall tremble and sorrow: for every

purpose of the Lord shall be performed against Babylon, to make the land of Babylon a desolation without an inhabitant" (Jer. 51:29 KJV). The spirit of Babylon is now in the process of being destroyed in the growing, maturing Christian. The Spiritual man will no longer dwell there or inhabit that realm, that is, operate from the carnal mind or from the influence of those systems. Eventually no man will reside there, or dwell in that corrupt system, for those systems will be destroyed.

The whole creation waits for the manifestation of the sons of God. (Ro. 8:19). It's an order of man being trained and fitted - and this will reach a perfect **man** by gradual growth and development, and that through the Word. To them it is given to know the mysteries of the kingdom (Mt. 13:11).

Man is purposed to grow in spirit as well as in the natural. In the natural, you grow from a babe, nourished on milk, into maturity, feasting on solid food. In the spirit you grow from a babe in Christ, on a diet of the milk of the Word, into youth, nourished on meat, and finally maturity, feasting on the hidden manna (Re. 2:17), which is Christ in you. It should be obvious that man (mankind), in order to mature into an overcoming adult, needs to digest more than the milk of the Word.

We read in 1 Sam. 20:24-25 (NAS): *"So David hid in the field; and when the new moon came, the king (Saul) sat down to eat food. And the king sat on his seat as usual, the seat by the wall; then Jonathan rose up and Abner sat down by Saul's side; but David's place was empty."* The wall represents the old system; Saul refused to budge away from that wall. A table is a type of a place of teaching and fellowship. Saul's table represents the old order, feasting on the milk of the Word, never any fresh present truth. David, of the new order, refused to eat at the king's table. Jonathan had just returned to his father's house. He is a type of those today starving for spiritual food, stunted in their growth, but unwilling to leave the old system and that bland, stale, food put before them. David's table, which Jonathan could eat from, has the fresh, solid food that Jonathan needed for spiritual growth.

God Chose Man

Man is the only creature of God to have superior intelligence and the only one who can personally know God or who can worship God. He is the only one who can receive the Spirit of God. He is the only creature who can give to God and Who will return. He is the only one who can develop a relationship with God and the only creature which can develop a spiritual relationship with each other. He is the only creature to receive God's (agape) love and the only one who can give that same love to others. **Man is the creature whom God has chosen in which to manifest Himself in the earth, first in His Only Begotten Son and now through the body of Christ**.

The many facets of God, His nature and His character, cannot be contained in one member of the body of Christ but is incased in all members - one major reason we need each other. God did not create robots but created each of us to come into the image of his creator, each a facet of His nature. Each of us can do one thing better than all the rest. Each of us in the body of Christ possesses a facet of the nature of God that the other members need and can rely on. Furthermore, His presence in the body is not a conglomeration of disjointed attributes nor randomly scattered fragments of divine nature, but a harmonious habitation (a result of His workmanship, Ep. 2:10), filled with the fullness of God (Eph. 3:11).

God's purpose for man is that He dwell in them. Ex. 25:8 KJV, *"And let them make me a sanctuary; that I may dwell among them." "..We are the temple of the living God. as God has said, I will dwell IN them and walk among them. I will be their God, and they shall be my people"* (2 Co. 6:16 NKJV).

The purpose of God is a man planted in His garden (Eden, Paradise, Kingdom) whose leaf shall not wither (Ps. 1:3). In Genesis God began with a man (Abraham) and ends with a people (Israel). In Psalms, we see that blessed is the man (Ps. 1:1) and blessed are all. *"...blessed are all that put their trust in him"* (Ps. 2:12).

Chapter 11

Man Must Grow Spiritually

It is inevitable that man, that is, spiritual man, will grow and mature into the image of God. God's universal law is in order - for plants, animals, natural man or spiritual man, that they should grow and mature and bear fruit, even seed within that fruit, and that seed should produce after its own kind for the following generations. The seed of Christ in the spirit filled person will produce after its own kind. Spiritual maturity will not happen in an instant or in a so-called literal rapture, for that does not follow God's pattern of growth

Jesus had just explained the parable of the sower, from which you can discern and understand all parables (Mk. 4:13) Mark 4:26-27 KJV, *"And he said, So is the kingdom of God, as if a man should cast seed into the ground; And should sleep, and rise night and day, and the seed should spring and grow up, he knoweth not how."* Verse 28 NKJV, *"For the earth yields crops by itself: first the blade then the head, after that the full grain in the head."* Verse 29 KJV *"But when the fruit is brought forth, immediately he putteth in the sickle, because the harvest is come."*

Verse 27 from Wuest- *"and should be sleeping and*

arising night and day, and the seed should be sprouting and lengthening, how, he does not himself know."

Nature's secret processes do not cease to operate just because we do not understand them. Like so, the mysterious growth of the kingdom of God in the hearts of believers is beyond the comprehension or understanding of the natural mind. Nevertheless that growth continues. The secret of that growth lies in the seed itself, whether we speak of a natural seed or the Seed of Christ. No principality or power in heaven or in earth can stop that growth of the Kingdom of God.

Quoting from Wuest Vol. 1 p. 92, "Just so, we sow the Seed (God's Word); the soil, namely the soul, receives it; the Holy Spirit works in the heart of the sinner, uses the seed sown and causes it to germinate and grow. This is the law and order in nature and also the law and order of grace in the Kingdom of God."

From Mk. 4:29. *"The harvest is come."* (Greek verb in perfect tense, indicating a process complete in past tense, having present results.)

It's the nature of plants, animals, natural man and spiritual man to grow and mature. You may sit in a service and receive life from the songs, from the sermon or some particular verse of Scripture. The person sitting next to you received no life and says, "I didn't get a thing." He may say or think, "Well, the seed (Word of God) I received was no good, it would not germinate in me." NO! There was nothing wrong with the seed. It just fell on poor or stony ground, It may not have been the right season for him (her).

Why are some saved in a given service and others are not. Is it the fault of the Seed they receive? NO! It's the fault of the ground. The seed has one hundred percent germination. Furthermore, it **will** grow and mature and reproduce itself. Someone may receive the Spirit of life from a certain verse on healing or on forgiveness, etc. Another reads the same verse and receives nothing. Is it the fault of the Seed (Word)? NO! The seed of Christ has one hundred percent germination.

With our natural mind we can discern nothing of what is going on inside of us spiritually. (1 Co. 2:14). Even with spiritual discernment or with the gift of knowledge or gift of wisdom we can discern only a fraction of what's going on inside ourselves or in others. Coming into maturity is a step by step process of development, every step in order. You know not how. We could not walk in what God was doing within us if we were conscious of all that went on within us. This would not be a faith walk and we are to walk by faith (2 Co. 5:7).

In the natural, growth continues - growth in our the cells of our body - they divide and multiply, old cells slough off. The same thing occurs spiritually. The kingdom of God is within you and is a dynamic, growing organism, never stagnant.

That seed **will** mature. Within that fruit is the seed for the next generation; That next generation is either people or situations. We just plant the seed (the Word of God). On a smaller scale, speak the word of God to a given problem or situation in your life. Go to bed at night, get up the next morning and go to work, go to bed that night, and get up again. Don't struggle, fret or worry about the seed and its growth. It will sprout and grow. It will produce according to its own kind.

In the natural, you don't go out every day and dig up the seed to see if it has sprouted. You will kill it. You wouldn't dissect a growing stalk of corn to see how it grows. Neither should we try to dissect our spiritual growth with our natural mind or natural logic. You know not how it grows. Just trust in God. You may say, "The Christian life is too difficult." You would like to give up and go another way. The corn plant can't say in the middle of its growth, "I don't want to be a corn plant, I'd rather be a radish."

Consider all of our involuntary muscles, that is, the muscles of our heart, liver, lungs, digestive system etc. If we had to consciously think about them in order to control and rule them, it would overwhelm us. We simply could not do it. Let us go one step further. If we had to consciously control and regulate, with our finite mind, the ten trillion cells of our body in their particular function, we could not begin to do it. But God is working in us. All we have to do is sleep, and rise night and day and trust God to take care of those details. By the same token, God is working on the spiritual activity within us. It is so detailed, we cannot discern it. Yes, we can sometimes see, we can look back over the past year and see some spiritual growth. But with our finite mind, we cannot control or measure that growth.

Fellowshipping with our brothers and sisters in the body of Christ, our spirit picks up strength, encouragement, comfort, correction, spiritual knowledge and spiritual food for growth that we cannot fully discern. We just go about our daily tasks, rise night and day. In the fullness of this fellowship there is a spiritual interaction then between members of the kingdom that we do not fully understand. With our finite mind, even with our renewed spiritual mind, we cannot comprehend this concept.

We are now in the process of manifestation. We will not wake up some day and suddenly be manifested Sons of God. The Christ within us does not progressively build up, strengthen and grow, in secret, as it were, then suddenly explode and manifest Himself in us. For one thing, we could not then walk in that nature. The Christ within us is already manifesting Himself, changing our lives, changing the way we walk, the way we think, the way we relate to God, the way we relate to our fellow believers and to the world, revealing the same Christ through us to others, in turn, changing their lives, bringing life to them. And it takes time to learn to walk in each of the changes in our lives as He manifests Himself in us and through us. Yes, God loves us the way we are, but He also loves us enough to want to help us grow, to change into His image.

How would you like it if God had, one, two or ten years ago, revealed to you all the processing that you would be going through up until now. It's by His grace that He does not., Instead, we have to walk it out by faith.

Eph. 4:14-15 NKJV, *"that we should no longer be children, tossed to and fro and carried about with every wind of doctrine, by the trickery of men, in the cunning craftiness of deceitful plotting, but, speaking the truth in love, may grow up in all things into Him who is the head; Christ."*

He. 6:1-2 NKJV, *"Therefore, leaving the discussion of the elementary principles of Christ, let us go on to perfection, not laying again the foundation of repentance from dead works and of faith toward God, of the doctrine of baptisms, of laying on of hands, of resurrection of the dead, and of eternal judgment."* The word "perfection" here from the Greek stresses the actual accomplishment of the end in view (Vine).

We read of the growth of Jesus. Lu. 2:40 KJV, *"And the child grew, and waxed strong in spirit, filled with wisdom: and the grace of God was upon him."* And in Lu. 2:52 KJV, *"And Jesus increased in wisdom and stature, and in favour with God and man."*

We grow through the Word. 1 Pe. 2:2, NKJV, *"as newborn babes, desire the pure milk of the word, that you may grow thereby,"* We are also admonished to grow in grace and knowledge (2 Pe. 3:18), in love (1 Th. 3:12), and in fruitfulness (2 Co. 9:10).

God does not allow us to do the things or act the same way we did last year, maybe even last month. He expects us to walk a straighter line, speak a purer, more positive language, to put away the childish things. He expects even our thought patterns and our attitude to be more holy. He expects us to walk more by the Spirit and less by sight. He expects us to bear more mature fruit. In short, He expects us to grow toward spiritual maturity.

One important characteristic of the seed is that it has the ability to reproduce itself (Ge. 1:12). Jesus Christ is that Seed within us, not seeds, but Seed (Ga. 3:16). Jesus Christ is not fragmented. The manifestation of the Person of Jesus Christ develops progressively within us. Moreover, that rate of growth differs from one individual to the next.

Order of Growth

The Holy Spirit uses the Seed sown (the Word of God) in a person, causes it to germinate and grow. This is a universal law in nature and an order in the Kingdom of God. God ordained, prescribed an order, first the seed, then the blade, then the head, then the full grain in the head, the 30, 60 and 100 fold realms, not the reverse. To advance from the outer court to Most Holy Place you must pass through the Holy Place. Salvation, Pentecostal Experience, then the Feast of Tabernacles Experience; the order is always the same. There is an order to growth for the individual and for the Body of Christ. The manifestation of a mature son does not come about by accident nor by random events but by proper divine growth along with an order to that growth.

Everything produces after or according to its own kind - plants, animals, the adamic or natural man and the spiritual man. An apple tree produces only apples, sheep produce only sheep. No matter how hard he tries, the natural man will never produce or manifest the true nature of God, the true love and the true character of God. Furthermore, the Christ in you, the incorruptible Seed of Christ, can manifest only one nature and that is the Christ nature. We can be assured that the Christ seed will not manifest an adamic nature, certainly not the nature of sheep or other animals or of the fallen man.

Yes, the incomplete man has two natures residing within him- the adamic nature and the Christ nature. Paul speaks of this in the seventh chapter of Romans. The world is waiting for the unveiling of that Christ nature in the Sons of God.

Let us say something about spiritual growth concerning the 30, 60 and 100 fold realms and setting goals. Don't get hung up on looking at the 99 fold realm. When you were in elementary school, you didn't fret or worry about what courses you would take or what you would be doing as a senior in college. Concerning the spiritual, in each area of your life, **in whatever realm or stage of that realm that you have mastered, be established in that truth, then get ready to move to the next realm.**

Chapter 12

Walking in Manifestation

The ungodly are those who do not know God in a personal way and exemplify an ungodly life style. The natural man never learns how to walk in peace, holiness, faith and victory. He obviously cannot conquer the flesh. He gets his guidance from his own experiences, and the counsel (advice) of the ungodly (Ps. 1:1). Oh, by world's standards many are successful. Yet until they are born again (born from above), they will not have access to divine guidance in their walk. Admittedly, for the child of God, it takes time to learn how to walk by faith, or how to be led by the Spirit - but it is a walk with God who gives perfect peace and in whose hands we can place our trust.

How do we walk in the Kingdom? Col. 2:6 Amp., *"As you have therefore received the Christ, (even) Jesus the Lord, [so] walk - regulate your lives and conduct yourselves - in union with and conformity to Him."* How did you receive Christ? Go back to verse 5 Amp., *"...in an orderly array and the firmness and the solid front and steadfastness of your faith in Christ, [that learning of the entire human personality on Him in absolute trust and confidence in his power, wisdom and goodness]."*

From Wuest's Expanded Translation, (v. *5-6*) *"...as you received Christ Jesus the Lord, in Him be constantly ordering your behavior..."* From Phillips, v. 6-7, *"Just as you received Christ Jesus the Lord, so go on living in Him - in simple faith. Grow out of him as a plant grows out of the soil it is planted in, becoming more and more sure of the faith as you were taught it, and your lives will overflow with joy and thankfulness."*

We see from these verses that by faith and trust, we receive Christ. It was not even our faith but His faith (Eph. 2:8-9).Then how do we walk or regulate and conduct ourselves in union with Him? By that same faith, trust and confidence in His power and in His wisdom.

Let us quote from Brother Bill Britton's book, *The Kingdom in Action,* regarding the Kingdom life. "This kingdom must not only be preached and entered, **but it must also be lived, be manifested to the world through the lives of His saints.** Some people seem to think that since they now have a higher revelation of the Word, that they don't have to live as holy as they did when they were under legalistic preaching. How wrong they are. This kingdom message and kingdom life brings a walk of holiness and purity that is as natural to the saints as breathing. There is no effort to producing righteousness when you have entered and are walking in the kingdom realm. It is your life".

Speaking of Titus 2:11, Bro. Bill continues, "So grace does not teach us that we can follow after the desires of the old man, or satisfy the craving of Adam's evil nature. Real grace teaches us to deny ungodliness and worldly lusts"

We must be committed to advance in God, despite the rough terrain. We can no longer be afraid to move on, because the nature of life is rooted in many different experiences, in many trials as well as mountain top experiences. Each previous realm and each previous step was needed to accomplish its purpose in us. **But we continue to walk in a new day, or new expression of Jesus Christ manifesting Himself in us and through us.** As we walk out each new truth revealed to us through Jesus Christ, God simply manifests one more aspect of His nature to first ourselves and then to the world.

To move on with God cannot be passive; we need to make a determined effort and consciousness toward that progress. Our walk will continually change as we move on and at times it will take adjustment on our part to that new step or gait. But it is *"God which worketh in you both to will and to do of His good pleasure"* (Phil. 2:13 KJV). And it is the Holy Spirit within us who is giving us the power to walk that walk. Not only that, but God gives us the desire, (will) to walk that walk. The Greek in this verse indicates this is a process of God working His thoughts in our lives to cause a change in our outward manifestation.

Paul wrote, *"I am crucified with Christ."* That inner working of the cross we so often would like God to take care of in one big moment, but God shows it to be a process. *"And he (Jesus) said to them all, If any man will come after me, let him deny himself, and take up his cross daily, and follow me"* (Lu. 9:23 KJV) - a daily, on-going process. Yet so many seek padded shoulders to carry the cross. Without a deep sense of commitment, a person tends to reject that daily grind of the cross, that chastening and processing in which God places them. To bear that cross in our walk we must die to all that is negative and to all selfishness. This death brings spiritual new life and allows us to eat spiritual food - the hidden manna.

Concerning the gathering of the manna, we read in Ex. 16:16 KJV, *"This thing which the Lord hath commanded. Gather of it every man according to his eating, an omer for every man, according to the number of your persons. Take ye every man for them which are in his tents."* We note here that each man had to gather for his own tent or household (our body or total being is our household). The lesson is this: we must commit to walk our own walk; we must walk out in our own life that which is revealed to us. Nobody is going to walk it out for us.

After Abraham separated from his family and Lot, God spoke to him. Gen. 13:14-15 KJV, *"And the LORD said unto Abram, after that Lot was separated from him, Lift up now thine eyes, and look from the place where thou art northward, and southward, and eastward, and westward: For all the land which thou seest, to thee will I give it, and to thy seed for ever."* And verse 17, *"Arise, walk through the land in the length of it and in the breadth of it; for I will give it unto thee."* And in Josh. 1:3, *"Every place that the sole of your foot shall tread upon, that have I given unto you, as I said unto Moses."*

Abraham saw a heavenly vision. But Joshua walked out the land. "Foot shall tread upon" speaks of conquering the enemy. "Feet" also speaks of understanding. It's not enough to see revelation by our spiritual eyes. To possess the land, we must walk it out, conquering the enemies as we go. Our enemies are not people but are spiritual, in our mind.

Josh. 11:23 KJV, *"So Joshua took the whole land, according to all that the LORD said unto Moses; and Joshua gave it for an inheritance unto Israel according to their divisions by their tribes. And the land rested from war.* " Whether our revelation comes to us as blessings or as corrections, we must walk them out. The blessings often come as a revelation to our spirit of our inheritance in the Kingdom.

We must commit ourselves to one another. We must realize we are not independent beings, each walking in the sphere of our own little kingdom. We must relate to one another in the body of Christ and to the ministries God places in our midst. We are members one of another, bone of His bone, and flesh of His flesh. Yes, We will become vulnerable to each other when we truly relate to one another. Many are reluctant to do that; learning to walk in harmony is not easy.

We Frame Our World

Eph. 3:20 KJV, *"Now unto him that is able to do (Amp.: carry out His purpose) exceeding abundantly above all that we ask or think (*Concordant Literal N.T.: *requesting or apprehending) according to the power that worketh in us."* V. 20. Wuest:, *"...in the measure of the power which is operative in us."* It is the Lord Jesus Christ who gives us the things above all that we ask.

Two important points here. First, that same power (*dunamis*) that raised Jesus from the dead works or actively operates within us to grant us, first of all, supernaturally, in a measure beyond what we are asking or beyond our imagination, **the ability to walk out** what we presently live in on a daily basis.

Second, relative to goals, that same power grants us the ability to spiritually see, and **to walk toward and to enter**

into spiritual dimensions far above and beyond what we could even imagine. The power of God working in our lives is limited only by our willingness to yield to Him. To that extent **We** determine **what** God can do for us or **what** we walk in.

We frame a world by what we speak, by how we act and by how we react. Whether we speak positive or negative, we still frame that positive or negative world. First, we need to get rid of the negative thoughts that hinder ourselves or others, and of the negative situations in our lives. Second, not only speak positive of our present situations, but positive beyond our present world, then begin to walk in that world. Could we also say that **you** determine **what** you walk in by what you think or speak. We, in most areas of our lives, live far below our God given potential. Thus, we need to enlarge our vision, or our coast, of where we can walk.

In the past we were taught to speak to that mountain (trouble), believe, then sit around and wait for God to act. More correctly, after we speak to that mountain and believe, we need to start walking toward that mountain. In other words, begin to walk and put those problems under our feet; begin walking in victory over our problems.

When you accepted Jesus Christ as your Saviour, you received a new nature, a divine nature (2 Pe. 1:4). That divine nature resides within you but it is not yet fully manifested. It begins with a seed. It's a process. At your new birth you begin to walk according to that new nature. You are not going to change your walk over night nor will you change it by your own strength and will power. You may try to and even succeed for a time, but you will fall back into your old pattern of bad habits and ungodly attitudes. You must rely on the power of the Holy Spirit (Acts 1:8) to change your walk. It is absolutely essential that you receive the baptism of the Holy Spirit, the earnest of our inheritance (Ep. 1:14) and that you move on into the third experience, the Feast of Tabernacles.

A Mature Walk

We must strive after Christ, resulting in a straighter, stronger walk, a walk of higher order. *"Until we all attain to the unity of the Faith and of the experiential, full, and precise knowledge of the Son of God, to a spiritually mature man, to the measure of the stature of the fullness of the Christ, in order that we no longer may be immature ones, tossed to and fro and carried around in circles by every wind of teaching in the cunning adroitness of men, in craftiness which furthers the scheming deceitful art of error, but speaking the truth in love, may grow up in Him in all things, who is the Head, Christ"* (Eph. 4:13-15 Wuest Expanded).

The word "perfect" from the KJV here is translated "spiritually mature" and comes from the Greek *Teileos* meaning complete, full age, mature. "Knowledge" comes from the Greek *epignosis* and denotes exact or full knowledge, discernment, recognition, a greater participation by the knower in the object known (W.E. Vine).

Spiritual maturity comes to a child of God, one moving toward sonship, only through trials, growth, time, and processing. By Hebrew tradition and scripturally the title "Son" was not decreed for a child until he was judged by the father to be spiritually mature. It was the father's duty to introduce the young lad as his son. It was not up to the son to proclaim it. Neither could the child claim to be a mature son by talking like his father or wearing his father's clothes. About Jesus, God declared, *"...Thou art My beloved Son, in whom I am well pleased"* (Mk. 1:11 KJV). This was not heard until Jesus was bout 30 years of age.

Your invitation is the life you live and the walk you walk, letting the Christ within you shine forth - in fact, shine forth so prominently, that people are attracted to you, really the Christ within you, and that you offer them spiritual food to eat, which is yourself. You have been tried in the fire, just as the fish and bread had been cooked by fire (Jn. 21:9). Are you ready to feed them, to give of yourself?

We read in Ro. 10:15 KJV, *"And how shall they preach, except they be sent? As it is written, How beautiful are the feet of them (plural) that preach the gospel of peace, and bring glad tidings of good things."* Paul is quoting from Is. 52:7 KJV which states, *"How beautiful upon the mountains are the feet of Him (singular) that bringeth good tidings."* Did Paul make a mistake? No! In Isaiah "Him" refers to Jesus Christ, the Head, whereas the "them" in Ro. 10:15 refers to the many membered body of Christ.

Does this verse speak of the beauty of literal feet? No! It refers to the way you walk in God, presenting Jesus Christ to the world. In other words, how beautiful is the walk of them that preach the gospel. This is not confined to pulpit preaching but speaks of all believers in the life they lead and live, the Christ they manifest to the world.

Jesus was the Word personified. If we are to follow His walk, then we demonstrate what the Word of God says; you walk that life. It's the life you live, the walk you walk. *"Always carrying about in the body the dying of the Lord Jesus, that the life of Jesus also may be manifested in our body. For we who live are always delivered to death for Jesus' sake, that the life of Jesus also may be manifested in our mortal flesh"* (2 Co. 4:10-11 NKJV).

Our mortal flesh is the nitty gritty of our daily life, what we do in our body, **our daily walk,** if you will. This is the bottom line - **that the life of Jesus may be manifested in our daily life, including our attitude and the way we act, think and talk.**

The Lord Jesus Christ guides us in a walk that is like His. How do we know what to do? We listen to His voice. He speaks to us in may ways - through His Word, through preaching, through others. He said, *"My sheep hear my voice, and I know them, and they follow me"* (Jn. 10:27). The Phillips translation reads, *"My sheep recognize my voice and I know who they are."* The Amplified: *"The sheep that are my own hear and are listening to My voice, and I know them and they follow Me."*

Here is a key- **a habit of listening**. It's an active process. You listen with an attentive spiritual ear and **expect** Him to speak. The unsaved scoff at the idea of believers hearing God speak to them but pay no attention to them. Just believe the Word. The Sons of God are those led by the Spirit of God (Ro. 8:14).

We Need Each Other

In the body of Christ you are unique. God needs you and the rest of the body needs you. Furthermore, God made us to need each other in order to exalt His name together

(Ps. 34:3). *"But so are they many members, yet but one body. And the eye cannot say unto the hand, I have no need of thee. Nor again the head to the feet, I have no need of you. Nay much more those members of the body, which seem to be more feeble, are necessary"* (1 Co. 12:20-22 KJV).

The Baptist cannot say to the Pentecostal, I have no need of thee, neither can the Pentecostal say to the Church of Christ member, I don't need you. The mature in Christ cannot say to the new born babe, "I have no need of you." Similarly, those walking in the 100 fold realm cannot say to those in the 30 fold realm, "I have no need of you."

We cannot say to another, "I don't understand your walk. I cannot see where you are walking. I can't keep step with you, therefore I can't (won't) walk with you." We may not all walk alike but we can walk in harmony and in love. We may not see eye to eye in doctrine but we can walk in love and in fellowship with one another. Each in the body of Christ has a unique walk. One in his walk has to overcome impatience, another stubbornness, another procrastination, another greed, another jealousy, or the works of the flesh. On the other hand, one is strong in gentleness, another in faithfulness, one in encouraging others, one in intercessory prayer, one brings peace to all they contact, another spreads joy. Each one of us needs the strengths of the others and we in turn need to share our strengths with them. Each one in the body of Christ possesses a unique facet of the nature of God of which they can reveal and share with the rest of the body and manifest to the world.

Like rough stones, each of us has rough edges that need to be rubbed off. That can only be done by those that come close to us. We need each other.

We may say that we believe that God will save any one. And we may claim to have the nature of God. Yet there are people we won't fellowship with or other people we would like to write off.

Walking in 30, 60 and 100 Fold Realms

Each (spiritual) territory in which we walk may require a different step, a different type of walk or gait. When we advanced from the Outer Court (30 fold realm) to the Holy Place (60 fold realm) we learned new steps, a new way to walk. We sought the Lord for guidance in this new walk. We no longer walk by natural light (understanding) but by the light of the candlestick (Holy Spirit). We have moved from the salvation experience to the Pentecostal experience. We had looked at Jesus as Saviour but now see the Christ, the Anointed. We came out of Egypt into a wilderness experience. We walked as workers but now walk as warriors. We no longer walk as children who drink milk but as more mature, eating bread. We advanced from walking in divine healing to walking in divine health. In this realm we no longer pay tithes but give tithes.

There are thirty major steps (31 to 60) to advance in the realm of the Holy Place. Likewise there are forty major steps (61 to 100) to advance in the realm of the Most Holy Place. Each step has a divine purpose, **each step a new experience of Jesus Christ manifesting Himself in us and through us to the rest of the body of Christ and to the world.**

There are no short cuts. You can't get from the Outer Court to the Most Holy Place without passing through the

Holy Place. And you can't go behind the veil without first passing the brazen altar. And from salvation, you cannot reach the Feast of Tabernacles experience without the Pentecostal experience. Likewise you cannot skip from step 32 to step 35. At step 32 you might catch a glimpse of and covet a resting place at 35 but you can't get there without taking steps 33 and 34. It's part of a process. We use these figures for illustrative purposes. We are not suggesting that you analyze yourself as to where you are located within the 30, 60 or 100 fold realms (Mt. 13:1-8). We certainly warn against trying to compare yourself to others as to where they are located spiritually along these areas.

There are those who desire to move on further with God. Take for example, one who has stepped out of the Pentecostal realm (31-60 fold) and into the kingdom realm (61- 100 fold). Some of these, you can see, when trouble comes, are walking at about only 61 or 62. Stepping beyond the veil, you still need to apply the blood, you're still 60 fold, you have not taken any steps of the 40 required (from 61 to 100). It is dark in there for you. Your eyes are still accustomed to the olive oil candle light of the Holy Place. But as you walk, sprinkling blood to the mercy seat, the light under the mercy seat starts to illuminate and begins to engulf the Most Holy Place. Divine light (understanding) then lights up your path.

As you step into that Most Holy Place, the brightness of the light of the candlestick (of the Holy Place) fades as you begin to walk in the divine light of the Shekinah. You walk now in the Feast of Tabernacles experience. You look to Jesus now as Lord more than the Christ. You walk out of the wilderness into the land. You walk as a worshipper rather than a warrior. You walk more like a mature son.

You have replaced your diet of bread with strong meat (solid nourishment - a deeper word). You walk more in divine life rather than divine health. You no longer give tithes; you are a tithe. Your walk emerges from the acceptable will of God to the perfect will of God.

Again, you seek the Lord for each step of the way, for it is a new walk. And again, you advance in the 100 fold realm by a process, beginning with step 61. You will not be perfected (become fully mature) until you have walked each step. And again, with each step Christ is manifesting Himself in a new way, in you and through you to the world.

Chapter 13

Fit for the Kingdom

In the ninth chapter of Luke we read the account of Jesus and three men who aspired to follow Him, but had excuses. To the first man he replied, *"The Son of Man has no place to lay His head."* (Lu. 9:58 KJV). Jesus was not feeling sorry for Himself because He had no permanent lodging place or a place to sleep at night. He was not worried about any such earthly desire. Jesus as the Head of the Body of Christ (Col. 1:18) as yet had no place or body of Christ (the church) or a permanent arrangement on which to lay His headship. (The foxes had holes and the birds had nests or permanent type homes). The cross lay between this point and the time when that body is formed. Jesus is in essence asking that man and us, are we willing to follow Him to the cross? Can we carry our own cross (Lu. 14:27)? Jesus had set His face to go to Jerusalem and to the cross.

What did Jesus mean, *"Let the dead bury their own dead?"* (Lu. 9:60 KJV). Partly, He means that the spiritually dead, including those stagnant in their spiritual growth, are taken up with earthly tasks and plans, awaiting natural death, for their horizon is limited - they cannot see perfection this side of the grave. If we are is to follow Jesus, we must forsake those things of the earth, (death realm) and proclaim the Kingdom of God.

In verse 62 KJV, He declared to one, *"... No man, having put his hand to the plow, and looking back, is fit for the kingdom of God."* Let us examine what this verse means.

"Having put his hand to the plow" speaks of commitment, persistence, constancy, dedication, determination and loyalty.

*"When all kinds of trials and temptations crowd into your lives, my brethren, don't resent them as intruders, but welcome them as friends! Realize that they come to test your faith and to produce in you the quality of endurance. **But let the process go on until that endurance is fully developed,** and you will find you have become men of mature character with the right sort of independence"* (Ja. 1:2-4 Phillips).

Paul wrote to the Philippians, *"I do not consider, brethren, that I have captured and made it my own [yet]; but one thing I do - it is my one aspiration: **forgetting what lies behind and straining forward to what lies ahead,** I press on toward the goal to win the [supreme and heavenly] prize to which God in Christ Jesus is calling us upward"* (Phil. 3:13-14 Amp.). Phillips translation: *"I leave the past behind and with hands outstretched to whatever lies ahead I go straight for the goal - my reward the honor of my high calling by God in Christ Jesus."*

"Forgetting what lies behind." Digging up hurts and problems of the distant past often does more harm than good. I believe in deliverance and the Scriptures back up the practice. But some people's past does not always call

for deliverance. We must get our focus off our problems and on to the solution. The problems then fade out of focus. How do we do that? By straining forward to what lies ahead.

From verse 13, "straining forward" or from the Revised, "stretching forward", is a metaphor of a foot race. In running a race, you don't look back to who or what is behind you, nor do you concern yourself with the spectators - those on the sidelines - some cheering, some jeering, and still others who keep insisting that you are headed in the wrong direction (following wrong teaching). You keep your eye on that goal.

In no sense in the race Paul describes does he suggest we are running from the enemy - always fighting or running from the devil as some do. Nor does it suggest we are trying to escape from something, such as our circumstances or the troubled world around us. It is not an escape from hell, nor is it an escape from our mortal bodies.

Forgetting What Lies Behind

What do we leave behind? First of all, we leave behind the old Adam and the kingdom of darkness. We leave behind aspects of our life before salvation - our course talk, negative talk, our living by the senses, bad habits and mannerisms. Admittedly, we may have some bad habits yet to overcome. We leave behind a hard or bitter spirit, our "stinkin thinkin", our holier than thou attitude and our sour attitude. We leave behind our tendency to measure or judge people (Zech. 2:1). We leave behind our failures and shortcomings, even the hurts of the past. We leave behind the memory of those angry words someone said to us, and learn to walk in forgiveness and love. We may even leave behind some of our activities, such as hobbies. We no longer wish we were back in that job, house, city or relationships we once cherished. We no longer cleave to the pleasant memories of the past.

"Do not say, 'Why is it that the former days were better than these?'" (Ecc. 7:10 NAS). *"When times are good, be happy; but when times are bad, consider: God has made the one as well as the other. Therefore, a man cannot discover anything about his future."* (Ecc. 7:14 NIV).

We no longer cling to old doctrines that we now have found to be false. We do not discount our experiences such as our family background, education, career etc., nor do we discount our salvation or Pentecostal experience. But we don't wish God would move again like He did in last week's service, in last month's revival or last year's convention, or how He moved in our individual lives in the past. In short, we don't discount those times but we move on with God.

As we strain forward to what lies ahead, to a greater and greater manifestation of God in our lives, we recognize that God does not allow us to do things that we did last year, maybe even last month. He is refining our holiness, cultivating our walk with Him. The trials and tribulations of the past we no longer see as stumbling blocks but as stepping stones to advance and strengthen our walk and the manifestation of God in our lives.

"Beloved, now we are the children of God, and it was not as yet manifested what we shall be. We are aware that, if He should be manifested, we shall be like Him, for we

shall see Him according as He is" (1 Jn. 3:2 Concordant Literal N.T.).

Jesus Christ is appearing or manifesting Himself in us right now to our spiritual eyes. As we appropriate each new manifestation or revelation of Christ, we see Him and we become more and more like Him (not physically but spiritually) each and every time. We no longer "look back," clinging to the vision of a physical Jesus, a babe in a manger. Neither do we leave Him hanging on a cross. His tomb is empty.

We are not waiting to see a six foot man Jesus drop out of the sky or wait till we "get to heaven" to see such a man walking down streets of gold. We see Him as He is. How is He now? He is the Ascended Christ, in spirit form, living in the hearts of believers. God is spirit. Jesus declared He was going back to the Father (Jn. 14:12). How? In spirit form.

The word "see" in the above verse comes from the Greek *optanomai* meaning to gaze (i.e. with wide-open eyes as at something remarkable). Contrast that with the Greek *theoreo*, meaning to be a spectator of, i.e. discern (lit., fig.). Notice this contrast in the usage found in John 16:6 KJV, *"A little while, and ye shall not see (*theoreo*) (naturally) me; and again a little while, and ye shall see (*optanomai*) (spiritually) me, because I go to the Father."*

When were the disciples to see Him again? In two thousand years or more? No! But in a little while. How did they see Him? In physical form? No! With their physical eyes? No! They would see the Ascended Christ with their spiritual eyes, the Ascended Christ **who has come again** - who came on the day of Pentecost - to dwell and live, not only in the disciples and others present, but within you and me today.

One who is fit for or appropriate for the kingdom has set a goal, running the race with perseverance. What was the goal which Paul sought? It was the resurrection out from among the dead, incorruption and eternal life, and that he might progressively know Jesus Christ, **that he might be transformed into the likeness of Jesus Christ.**

Let's read Phil. 3:10-12 from the Amplified: *"[For my determined purpose is] that I may know Him - that I may progressively become more deeply and intimately acquainted with Him, perceiving and recognizing and understanding [the wonders of His person] more strongly and more clearly. And that I may in that same way come to know the power outflowing from His resurrection [which exerts over believers]; and that I may so share His suffering as to be **continually transformed [in spirit into His likeness even] to His death**, [in the hope] that if possible I may attain to the [spiritual and moral] resurrection [that lifts me] out from among the dead [even while in the body]. Not that I have now attained [this ideal] or am already made perfect, but press on to lay hold of (grasp) and make my own, that for which Christ Jesus, the Messiah, has laid hold of me and made me His own."*

The KJV in Phil. 3:21 reads, *"Who shall change our vile body, that it may be fashioned like unto his glorious body, according to the working whereby he is able even to subdue all things unto himself."* Here the Greek for "change" is *metaschematizo.* We contrast this with *metamorphoo* meaning change into another form (*morphe*), as a caterpillar to a butterfly, and used of Christ's transfiguration and in Ro. 12:2 *"be ye transformed (METAMORPHOO) by the renewing of your mind"*

The former Greek word comes from the noun *schema* translated often as "fashion" as in 1 Co. 7:31, "...fashion of this world, signifying that which comprises the manner of life, actions etc. of humanity in general." In Ph. 2:8 the Lord being found in "fashion" (*schema*) as a man or what He was in the eyes of man.

The noun *morphe* thus relates more to the inward man, and *schema* to the outward man or outer appearance. We are in that body of humiliation and our outward man is being changed into the body of His glory.

We now have that power within us - we are being changed. What this verse speaks of is a change to a Christ like nature, even His glorified body, that people will recognize the Christ that is within us, will identify us as a citizen of heaven that we are, and see us not bearing the language and mode of life of the man of the earth.

Words of Jesus Are Life

Jesus said, *"It is the Spirit that gives life - He is the life-giver; the flesh conveys no benefit whatsoever - there is no profit in it. **The words (truths) that I have been speaking to you are spirit and life**"* (Jn. 6:63 Amp.). He also spoke words of life to the scribes and Pharisees. If they would have accepted Him, His words would have burned the death of hypocrisy out of them and begun to clean and purge them.

What we wish to emphasize here is that in each and every one of the statements of Jesus, no matter how simple on the surface, He spoke **Life**, that is, spiritual life. The words that Jesus spoke had not only spiritual meaning for the moment in which He spoke but beyond - into this age and the ages to follow.

As sons of God, training to be fit for the kingdom, we should learn to speak nothing but life. Just eliminating idle and vain talk is not enough. From Rev. 14:5, *"And in their mouth was found no guile: for they are without fault before the throne of God."* The Amp.: *"No lie was found to be upon their lips."* We must not think or speak wrong or condemnation of any one, even ourselves.

As we speak life, we will bring life to all creation. Creation groans for this life. We will speak from the fullness - from the life of Jesus Christ Who is within us. When sons become fully manifested, they will have followed the Pattern Son, never to falter in their walk or talk, and will be speaking life by every utterance of their lips.

Chapter 14

When Is Such
A Manifestation Expected?

The adamic man, possessing the nature of the fallen man, cannot be improved upon. But man receives a new nature via the rebirth from above. Thus he is a new creature (2 Co. 5:17). To the extent that the regenerated man walks with God and has progressed in God, has been transformed by the renewing of his mind (Ro. 12:2), he can manifest that very same divine nature, right now, right here on the earth. That is the Jesus Christ that others and the world will see. *"And I have declared unto them thy name (nature), and will declare it: that the love wherewith thou hast loved me may be in them, and I in them"* (Jn. 17:26 KJV).

1 Co. 15:47-48 NIV, *"The first man was of the dust of the earth, the second man from heaven. As was the earthy man, so are those who are of the earth; and as is the man from heaven, so also are those who are of heaven."*

Let Us Bear the Image

Continuing in 1 Co. 15:49 from the Amp., *"And just as we have borne the image of the (man) of dust, so* **shall we**

and so let us bear the image of the (Man) of heaven."
Concordant Literal N.T. *"And according. as we bear the
image of the soilish (spelled correctly, NOT 'soulish'), we
should be wearing the image also of the Celestial."* Greek
Interlinear:, *"And as we bore the image of the earth man,
we shall bear the image of the heavenly man."* Wuest:
*"And even as we bore the derived image of that which is
earthly, we shall also bear the derived image of that which
is heavenly."*

The word "bear" comes from the Greek *phoreo*,
meaning not a simple act of bearing but a continuous or
habitual condition.

It was easy for us, before we were saved, to bear the
image of the earthy, for that was our nature. It was easy to
live by the senses, to live as the world lives. It was easy to
sin, (some of our sin was habitual) for that was our nature.
Then "according as" or in the same manner, we bear the
image of the heavenly, that is, the Person of Jesus Christ.
How? By His nature that dwells within us and the Holy
Spirit that empowers us to live that life.

When do we bear that heavenly image? We are not
speaking of the sweet by and by, but **now** as we put on the
Lord Jesus Christ. God is forming a people into the image
and likeness of His Son, Jesus Christ, a people who speak
life and who walk out and live the life of which they speak,
a people who walk out in shoe leather, that is, in the
everyday activity of their lives, the very character and
attributes of the Lord Jesus Christ.

Instead of moving by the senses and by the dictates of
the flesh, we begin to be led and move by the Spirit (Ro.
8:14). Every basic move, channel of thought and line of
action, to the extent we yield to Him, is finally affected by

that new personality within us, that of the Lord Jesus Christ. If we allow Him, there is no part of our being, our every day life, even the thoughts and intents of our heart that the Person of Jesus Christ cannot touch and influence, bringing us to bear the very image of Him.

So many Christians and much of the world see Jesus only as a babe in a manger or as the sacrificial Lamb on the cross, or a historical Jesus, or they look for His physical appearance in the natural clouds, or they postpone everything of Jesus until some distant future. But now is the time. The world groans **now** for the manifestation of Jesus Christ in and through the sons of God. The vehicle in which God purposes to carry out His will, in which He is manifested to the world is the (true) church, the ecclesia, the called out ones.

The Sons and the Multitude

Mt. 15:29-31 KJV, *"And Jesus departed from thence, and came nigh unto the sea of Galilee; and went up into a mountain, and sat down there. And great multitudes came unto him, having with them those that were lame, blind, dumb, maimed, and many others, and cast them down at Jesus' feet; and he healed them: Insomuch that the multitude wondered, when they saw the dumb to speak, the maimed to be whole, the lame to walk, and the blind to see: and they glorified the God of Israel."*

To sit down speaks of a position of authority. How did the blind get to the mountain top? Someone had to lead them. This speaks of the spiritually blind today. The people of the world are hungry for life (which one finds on a mountain top - or the mountain speaks of a higher place in

God.). But because they are blind, they are looking in the wrong place - to the things of the world. They are waiting for the manifestation of God. They need the sons of God to lead them.

The lame speaks of spiritually lame people, those who cannot walk out what they see spiritually. How did they get up the mountain? They were either carried or they crawled - speaks of extra effort. Again, they need the sons of God to help them walk. The "dumb" indicates those today who are unable to speak the words of life or truth, words that line up with the Word of God.

Mt. 15:35-36 KJV, *"And he commanded the multitude to sit down on the ground. And he took the seven loaves and the fishes, and gave thanks, and brake them, and gave to his disciples, and the disciples to the multitude."*

The sons of God in manifestation will command the multitude to sit - where there is rest in God. Sons, as Jesus did, focus not on the few loaves and fishes but on what God is going to produce, on the expansion of the kingdom. I believe Jesus did not give thanks for the few fishes but instead prayed something like this:"Heavenly Father, I thank you that you have given me power and authority over all the bread of the land and all the fish of the seas - to call them into being to feed these people, that they be fed in full abundance (Jn. 10:10) with some left over."

We must not focus on the three fishes or our tithes or offering or on the sweat we produce for the kingdom, but on what God will do and how He will work. Jesus did not concentrate on the seed planted in the earth but on the much fruit (Jn. 12:24). God gave His only begotten Son - for a purpose - that whosoever believeth in Him should not perish but have everlasting life.

Mt. 14:15-20 KJV, *"And when it was evening, his disciples came to him, saying, This is a desert place, and the time is now past; send the multitude away, that they may go into the villages, and buy themselves victuals. But Jesus said unto them, They need not depart; give ye them to eat.*

And they say unto him, We have here but five loaves, and two fishes. He said, Bring them hither to me. And he commanded the multitude to sit down on the grass, and took the five loaves, and the two fishes, and looking up to heaven, he blessed, and brake, and gave the loaves to his disciples, and the disciples to the multitude. And they did all eat, and were filled: and they took up of the fragments that remained twelve baskets full."

Jesus never called the multitude to Him. When the sons are ready, we will go to the multitude. Neither did Jesus feed the multitude. (V. 19) That's for the sons to do. But if we are not broken before we go to the multitude, we will be so full of pride, we will be like moldy bread, void of life. They did eat and **all** were filled. This speaks of a pattern or type for all mankind to eat the spiritual food of the kingdom and be filled. Bread speaks of the Word of God and of life. The two fishes are the sign of the Lord Jesus Christ.

An Order in God

Within the confines or sphere of the manifested sons, there is an order and rule for them to follow. You remember the familiar story of the centurion who wanted Jesus to heal his servant. From Mt 8:7-9 KJV, *"And Jesus saith unto him, I will come and heal him. The centurion answered and said, Lord, I am not worthy that thou shouldest come under my roof: but speak the word only, and my servant shall be healed. For I am a man under authority, having soldiers under me: and I say to this man, Go, and he goeth; and to another, Come, and he cometh; and to my servant, Do this, and he doeth it."*

The NKJV adds, *"For I **also** am a man under authority."* The centurion recognized two things. First, that Jesus submitted to the higher authority of God, and second, because He did, He had authority over disease and sickness, which was of a lower realm than the words of life of Jesus.

As the sons of God submit to the authority of Jesus Christ, they, too, will be granted authority to rule and reign over things of a lower nature, such as sickness, disease, the kingdoms of this world, over their own flesh, and over evil spirits. Any child of God can do this now.

The spirit man, coming into the realm of the spirit, is going to rule and reign with Jesus Christ over all creation - plants, animals, nature, and the souls of men, because he will have that power and that authority. *"Now unto him that is able to do exceeding abundantly above all that we ask or think, **according to the power that worketh in us**"* (Eph. 3:20).

Jesus did not cease His work when He left the earth realm. What is to be accomplished in this age and the eons to come will be accomplished through a many membered Christ, the ascended Christ, indwelling and working in and through His saints (Jn. 14:20; Col. 2:19; 1 Co. 12:27)

Now Is the Time

When is this reality coming to pass? **Now!** It's been

going on in increasing intensity the past decades. God seeks to manifest the nature of Himself through Jesus Christ in a people now. You ask, "Why hasn't it been done the past 2000 years?" It has to a small extent, in a remnant, but the time was not ready.

We have established that the manifestation (*apokalupsis*) of the Sons of God or the manifestation of God in the sons means the unveiling or revealing of God in the sons. We might compare the unveiling of Christ with that of a sculpture or painting or other work of art. Before the public unveiling, the art work is already finished and in place. It does not have to be brought from some other location nor does the public see, at the unveiling, a person still painting or chiseling away at a piece of stone or marble. That object has to be there to be seen or unveiled.

Now Jesus already dwells in the hearts of believers. (Col. 1:27; 1 Co. 3:16-17; 6:19; Jn. 17:23; Jn. 14:23) We have discussed this previously. In order for Him to be revealed, we don't have to wait for Him to come from some other location, such as out in the sky, or even from another dimension. He is in place and He is complete. Neither does He need to change His form. He is in the form of the Spirit of Jesus Christ or the Spirit of God. He cannot be seen with the natural eye. But He manifests His nature and character in the lives of the believers, especially the sons of God who are led by the spirit.

The unveiling has taken place. We do not yet see the fullness of the nature of Christ in the body of Christ but as we have discussed, each member in the body of Christ already manifests unique aspects of that nature in their daily lives. As each individual grows and as the body of Christ grows, so the revealing become clearer and clearer in both the individuals, in the total body of Christ and to the world. This is happening now. It's not some future event on the calendar. If we continue to futurize this unveiling or manifestation, it is nothing more than a glorified rapture.

We are now in the third thousand-year-day since Christ, the seventh since Adam (2 Pe. 3:8; Hos. 6:2; Lu. 13:22; Jn. 2:19). Today is the day the temple of The Lord is to be raised. We are coming into the cycle of the seventh day from Adam, the third from the cross or birth of Jesus. According to how you count years (Bible scholars differ), we are in that millennial reign now or beginning it. We are in that frame of time when the manifestation of the Sons of God should be occurring. There is a manifestation of the Sons of God. The world is coming to the realization that Saviors have to come and rescue this world. God will move only through His sons. There are people now who are walking in the heavenlies, releasing creation, reconciling all men back to the Father.

Now, in the time in which we live, we witness the manifestation or the unveiling of the sons of God. The corporate son is now rising from the darkness of the earthly realm into the brightness of the heavenly realm, and is one in whom all the world can see and perceive the nature and character of God. But it will take one thousand years for the manifestation to be completed because we are dealing with a corporate man.

Bibliography

Britton, Bill, *The Church in Action,* P.O. Box 707, Springfield, Mo 65801 Not copyrighted.

Vine, W. E. *An Expository Dictionary of New Testament Words*, Fleming Revell Co.

Wuest, Kenneth S., *Wuest's Word Studies from the Greek New Testament*, Wm. B. Eerdmans Pub. Co., Grand Rapids MI 49502. Copyright 1940,1941,1942,1945,1952, by Wm. B. Eerdmans Co.

Additional copies of this book may be purchased from:

OMEGA

Richard W. Rundell
P.O. Box 983
Haskell, OK 74436-0983
(918) 482-5066

FOR ADDITIONAL COPIES WRITE:

Impac *Chris* *ian* *Books*

332 Leffingwell Ave., Suite 101
Kirkwood, MO 63122

AVAILABLE AT YOUR LOCAL BOOKSTORE, OR YOU MAY ORDER DIRECTLY. Toll-Free, order-line only M/C, DISC, or VISA 1-800-451-2708.